Gronlund's Writing Instructional Objectives

Gronlund's Writing Instructional Objectives

Eighth Edition

Norman E. Gronlund

Professor Emeritus,
University of Illinois at Urbana–Champaign

Susan M. Brookhart

Duquesne University

PEARSON

Merrill
Prentice Hall

Upper Saddle River, New Jersey
Columbus, Ohio

Library of Congress Cataloging-in-Publication Data

Gronlund, Norman Edward, 1920-
  Gronlund's writing instructional objectives / Norman E. Gronlund, Susan M. Brookhart. —
8th ed.
      p. cm.
  Includes bibliographical references and index.
  Rev. ed. of: Writing instructional objectives for teaching and assessment. 2004.
  ISBN-13: 978-0-13-175593-2
  ISBN-10: 0-13-175593-5
    1. Lesson planning. 2. Education—Aims and objectives. I. Brookhart, Susan M.
    II. Gronlund, Norman Edward, 1920—Writing instructional objectives for teaching and
assessment. III. Title.
  LB1027.4.G76 2009
  371.3'028—dc22

                                                                            2007040286

Vice President and Executive Editor: Jeffery W. Johnston
Publisher: Kevin M. Davis
Acquisitions Editor: Bill Larenson
Editorial Assistant: Lauren Reinkober
Director of Marketing: Quinn Perkson
Marketing Manager: Erica M. DeLuca
Marketing Coordinator: Brian Mounts
Production Manager: Wanda Rockwell
Creative Director: Jayne Conte
Cover Design: Bruce Kenselaar
Cover Illustration/Photo: Getty Images
Full-Service Project Management/Composition: Nitin Agarwal, Aptara, Inc.
Printer/Binder: Courier/Stoughton

Credits and acknowledgments borrowed from other sources and reproduced, with
permission, in this textbook appear on appropriate page within text.

Pearson Education LTD.
Pearson Education Australia PTY, Limited
Pearson Education Singapore, Pte. Ltd
Pearson Education North Asia Ltd
Pearson Education, Canada, Ltd
Pearson Educación de Mexico, S.A. de C.V.
Pearson Education–Japan
Pearson Education Malaysia, Pte. Ltd

10 9 8 7 6 5 4 3 2 1
ISBN-13: 978-0-13-175593-2
ISBN-10:   0-13-175593-5

To
Marie Ann Gronlund
and
Erik, Derek, and David

To
Frank, Carol, and Rachel

Preface

This book provides a practical approach to writing objectives as intended learning outcomes. We describe and illustrate how to state instructional objectives in terms of the types of performance students must demonstrate to show that they have achieved the goals of instruction. We show how instructional objectives can be derived from state standards. The procedure can be used with all types of learning outcomes and is especially useful with complex learning outcomes such as thinking skills, performance skills, and problem solving.

We stress the important role of objectives in the teaching–learning–assessment process. The text shows how well-written instructional objectives contribute to more effective instruction and improved student learning.

Part I describes how to get started in writing instructional objectives, how to use objectives in planning for instruction and assessment, how content standards can serve as a general framework for writing objectives, and some factors to consider in preparing instructional objectives.

Part II describes and illustrates how to write objectives for cognitive learning outcomes (ranging from knowledge to thinking skills), affective outcomes, and two levels of performance outcomes (traditional performance skills and problem-solving skills).

Part III describes and illustrates how to use instructional objectives in the construction and interpretation of achievement tests and in the assessment of performance and affective outcomes.

This edition differs from the last edition in the following ways:

1. The objectives at the beginning of each chapter are written in the format of Gronlund Instructional Objectives. As such, they identify what readers should understand and be able to accomplish after reading the chapter.

2. We added exercises at the end of each chapter that reflect a sample of the specific learning outcomes for that chapter. Appendix F provides the answers to the exercises.

3. Throughout the book, we have added information about how instructional objectives are used with formative as well as summative assessment.

4. Chapter 4 describes the use of state content standards as a basis for writing instructional objectives. New examples from six different states illustrate this process.

5. Chapter 5 presents two new frames of reference for preparing instructional objectives. The 2001 revision of Bloom's Taxonomy is included; this framework is also covered in most current educational psychology textbooks. The Webb Depth of

Knowledge levels are also included. Because the Webb framework is currently used in many states for studies of the alignment of state assessments and state standards, it is an important frame of reference for the instructional objectives intended to teach those standards.

These improvements in the book should add to its usefulness as a guide for writing instructional objectives and using them in teaching and assessment.

Our special thanks to the reviewers for their suggestions for desirable changes: John Michael Bodi, Bridgewater State College; Robert Carrier, University of Michigan; Fred Ramirez, California State University, Fullerton; and Gary Todd Vanek, Washington State University. Thanks also go to Calvin K. Claus for the list of verbs in Appendix E, and to the editorial staff of Merrill/Prentice Hall.

S. M. B.
N. E. G.

Contents

NOTE: Every effort has been made to provide accurate and current Internet information in this book. However, the Internet and information posted on it are constantly changing, so it is inevitable that some of the Internet addresses listed in this textbook will change.

Gronlund's Writing Instructional Objectives

Part I

Preparing Instructional Objectives

Chapter 1

Focusing on Intended Learning Outcomes

INSTRUCTIONAL OBJECTIVE:

Understands the purposes and uses of general instructional objectives and specific learning outcomes.

1. Describes what is meant by stating instructional objectives as intended learning outcomes.
2. Describes the differences between objectives at the training level and objectives for higher-level learning outcomes.
3. Describes the advantages of using instructional objectives that are stated as intended learning outcomes.
4. Distinguishes between objectives stated as learning outcomes and those stated in terms of the teaching process or the learning process.
5. Explains why it is desirable to include both general objectives and specific learning outcomes when writing instructional objectives.
6. States reasons for not including standards when writing instructional objectives.

When you think about planning for instruction, you might think first about organizing your content, teaching method, and materials. These are all important elements of instructional planning, but the entire process is more effective if you first consider instructional objectives. What are the intended *learning outcomes* of the instruction? How can you describe, in performance terms, what students are like when they have learned what is expected of them? Clarifying your intended learning outcomes provides a basis for instructional planning and sets the stage for both teaching and assessment.

Instructional Objectives as Intended Learning Outcomes

You can state instructional objectives in many ways. For example, you might state them in terms of the teaching procedure, as follows:

1. Teach students the terms used on weather maps.
2. Demonstrate to students the construction of a weather map.

Another way to state objectives is in terms of the learning process, as follows:

1. Students learn the terms used on weather maps.
2. Students learn how weather maps are constructed.

These two ways describe what the teacher is doing and what the students are learning, but neither method describes the intent of the instruction or the learning. What can students do to show that they have learned what was expected of them? Do you want them to define the weather terms, to relate them to weather symbols, to use them in written weather descriptions, or what? After students have learned how weather maps are constructed, are they expected to construct weather maps or simply interpret them? The problem of stating objectives in terms of teaching procedure or student learning is that the *goals* or *targets* of instruction are not clear.

A more useful way to state instructional objectives is in terms of the intended learning outcomes of the instruction. This makes clear the types of student performance you are willing to accept as evidence that the students have learned what was expected of them. Thus, for our example on weather, you might state the objectives as follows:

1. Defines the meaning of the weather terms in his or her own words.
2. Relates the terms to symbols used on a weather map.
3. Describes the features of a weather map using relevant terms.
4. Interprets weather conditions at various locations on a weather map.

When stated in this manner, the objectives clarify what students can do to demonstrate that they have learned. This provides the goals or targets of instruction in terms of measurable or observable student performance. Stated as intended learning outcomes, they provide a focus for instruction and provide a basis for the assessment of student achievement.

This book, then, will describe and illustrate how to write instructional objectives as intended learning outcomes that provide effective goals for teaching and targets for assessment. Instructional objectives are an important component of the teaching–learning–assessment process. Before you select teaching procedures and instructional materials, it is important to know what you want the students to achieve. Everything you do in the classroom is directed toward improving student learning, but how do you know when they have learned? If you focus on course content only, you are apt to overemphasize the recall of factual information, which has been done so frequently in the past. What about the comprehension of concepts, the application of concepts and principles, problem-solving skills, reasoning ability and other higher-level learning outcomes? If you expect achievement in these areas, you should be able to clarify in performance terms what students can do to show that they have achieved these expected learning outcomes.

Levels of Goals and Objectives

The intended outcomes of education can be stated in broad general terms as is necessary in stating national, state, or school goals (e.g., demonstrates proficiency in basic skills), or they can be stated in more specific terms for instructional purposes. Our focus will be on the writing of instructional objectives that provide a focus for teaching, learning, and assessment. The statement of instructional objectives will vary somewhat, however, depending on the nature of the instruction.

Objectives at the Training Level

Training programs typically require objectives that are specific, limited, and well defined. These specific objectives are frequently stated as tasks to be performed rather than as goals to work toward. Thus, we might have statements such as the following:

Adds single-digit whole numbers.

Identifies the parts of a microscope.

Lists the steps in preparing a bar graph.

The teaching emphasis is on modifying and shaping student behavior to fit these predetermined task descriptions. There is a one-to-one relation between the stated objective, the teaching procedure, and the testing procedure. For example, we want students to be able to add whole numbers, we teach them to add whole numbers, and we test them by having them add whole numbers. Thus, the specific objective is stated as a task, the task is directly taught, and the task is directly tested, as shown in Figure 1.1.

This model is widely used in training programs and for some simple learning outcomes in classroom instruction. However, it is inappropriate for more complex learning outcomes. Unfortunately, these specific behavioral objectives were once the focus of classroom instruction. This resulted in long, unmanageable lists of specific objectives that emphasized simple knowledge and skill outcomes to the neglect of more complex learning outcomes.

Figure 1.1   The Teaching–Learning–Assessment Sequence

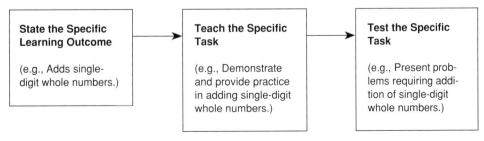

State the Specific Learning Outcome	**Teach the Specific Task**	**Test the Specific Task**
(e.g., Adds single-digit whole numbers.)	(e.g., Demonstrate and provide practice in adding single-digit whole numbers.)	(e.g., Present problems requiring addition of single-digit whole numbers.)

With the increasing emphasis in education on comprehension, reasoning, problem solving, the application of learning to "real-life" situations, and other complex learning outcomes, the listing of specific tasks is inadequate for describing the vast array of intended outcomes of education.

The specific learning tasks used in classroom instruction are, of course, derived from the objectives, but they typically provide the means to an end rather than serve as ends in themselves. For example, we certainly do want students to be able to add, but the goal is not simply skill in addition. The ultimate goal is that students comprehend the concept of addition and understand its use in solving different types of problems. You really care that students not only know how to do addition, but also understand when to use it and why it is being used. Similarly, you may teach students new vocabulary, but the intended outcome is improved reading, writing, or speaking, and not simply increased vocabulary. The instructional objectives provide the focus for instruction and the specific learning tasks provide the activities designed to achieve the intended learning outcomes. With simple learning outcomes the objectives and tasks may be similar, but with complex learning outcomes they are likely to differ considerably.

Objectives for Higher-Level Learning Outcomes

Advances in cognitive psychology have supported a shift away from stating objectives in terms of the specific learning tasks to be mastered, toward a more holistic approach focused on complex learning outcomes. Thinking, reasoning, and complex problem solving can occur at all levels of learning if students are actively engaged in constructing meaning from their experiences. Instead of the sequential achievement of specific learning tasks from simple to complex, you want students to show more integrated learning, with a broader emphasis on problem solving, reasoning, thinking skills, and other complex types of performance outcomes. This approach also favors the use of comprehensive tasks more like those in the real world (e.g., how to reduce water pollution). Obviously, with this approach to teaching, learning, and assessment, you cannot reduce the objectives to a list of simple tasks to be mastered. Rather, your statements of learning intentions focus on the more complex outcomes (e.g., uses mathematical concepts in describing a problem). The teaching and testing of specific tasks is replaced by greater emphasis on holistic learning and performance assessment of the more complex learning outcomes. Almost all students can achieve these higher-level learning outcomes regardless of grade level or achievement background, if they have proper instruction.

A holistic approach to learning does not eliminate the need for a clear statement of our intended learning outcomes. The current emphasis on educational accountability requires a clear focus on expected achievement and the means of assessing it, so that the effectiveness of instructional programs can be determined.

For complex learning outcomes, the instructional objectives are more general than those at the training level. Rather than being stated as specific tasks, each objective represents a whole class of responses (e.g., comprehends concepts). Because of their general nature, you typically need to define them further in terms of student performance. For example, comprehension of concepts might be shown by having students define them in their own words, give examples of them, and describe the similarities and differences between them.

The more complex the objective, the more crucial—and more difficult—it is to communicate the learning target to students. However, it must be done! Students have no chance of achieving an objective if they don't know what it is. You must communicate the learning target to students, help them compare their performance to that target, and suggest strategies they can use for improvement.

This is called formative assessment. Although formative assessment is also used in the teaching–learning–assessing sequence for training objectives, it becomes more important for higher-level learning objectives. With objectives beyond the training level the one-to-one relationship between the stated objective, the teaching procedure, and the assessment procedure is no longer appropriate. The objectives provide goals for teaching and targets for assessment, but the teacher is free to use a variety of methods and materials in helping students to achieve the objectives. Thus, the objectives provide direction for both the teacher and the students without being overly restrictive about the nature of the instruction or the types of learning activities students engage in. Objectives for higher-level learning outcomes permit an openness and exploration in the instructional process that is absent in the closely prescribed shaping and molding process characteristic of the training level.

A variety of learning experiences is not only possible at the higher levels of learning but it is also necessary. To develop a comprehension of concepts, for example, you might need to use questioning strategies that challenge students' misconceptions, problem-solving projects, direct experience with situations, and oral or written reports. Thus, the relation of objectives to teaching and assessment at this level is illustrated in Figure 1.2.

The student performances described in Step 1 provide the basis for selecting learning activities and providing feedback and strategies in Step 2 and the assessment procedures in Step 3. With higher-level learning outcomes the focus is on integrated response patterns rather than specific and limited learning tasks.

The method of stating objectives in this book is in terms of the intended learning outcomes of instruction and is not tied to any particular instructional method. The stated objectives simply indicate the types of performance you are willing to accept as evidence of achievement. This method of stating objectives is applicable to all types of student performance ranging from simple to complex, and is especially useful with the higher levels of learning outcomes now being stressed in education. In short, it describes the intended outcomes of instruction in performance terms without restricting the means of achieving them.

Figure 1.2   Relationship of Objectives to Teaching and Assessment

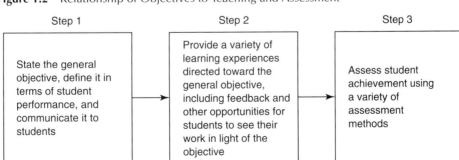

Uses of Instructional Objectives

When instructional objectives are properly stated as intended learning outcomes they serve a number of useful purposes, as shown in Figure 1.3.

Figure 1.3 illustrates that objectives can be useful in teaching, student learning, assessment, informing others of your instructional intent, and evaluating the effectiveness of your instruction. We discuss each of these uses in turn.

Role of Objectives in Teaching

Stating your objectives as intended learning outcomes provides a basis for selecting the methods and materials of instruction that are most likely to bring about these changes. If you want students to comprehend concepts, you have to select those instructional techniques and materials that help students form the proper conceptions and eliminate common misconceptions. If you want students to develop reasoning ability, you have to

Figure 1.3   Uses of Instructional Objectives

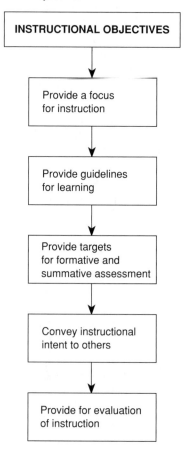

provide experiences that require the use of reasoning. If you want students to be able to solve problems like those in the real world, you have to plan for projects that require the solving of realistic complex problems. Instructional objectives that are stated clearly in performance terms provide a framework for planning the type of instruction needed to bring about the desired outcomes.

Instructional objectives also provide a basis for integrating teaching, learning, and assessment. These should all be in close harmony. For example, in planning for problem-solving outcomes, the instructional activities and assessment procedures must be in close agreement with the intended outcomes described in the objective. This provides a common focus for monitoring learning progress, guiding student learning, and determining end-of-instruction achievement. In a well-planned teaching–learning–assessment program the three phases of instruction are barely distinguishable from one another. All are directed toward the same intended learning outcomes and all have a common purpose—improved student learning.

Instructional objectives also provide a basis for providing feedback to students. If you describe your intended outcomes clearly enough, you can pinpoint learning strengths and weaknesses and provide students with timely and clear guides for improving learning. For example, if you describe problem-solving outcomes in sufficient detail, you can determine whether students can distinguish between accurate and inaccurate data, facts and opinions, or relevant and irrelevant events. If not, you can plan remedial work to overcome the deficiencies.

Role of Objectives in Student Learning

If you share instructional objectives with students at the beginning of instruction, they give students clear achievement targets to work toward and clarify the purpose of the various learning activities. This is motivating to students and it also makes clear to them the complexity of the learning process. When they understand that learning will include not only knowledge outcomes, but reasoning, problem solving, and various performance skills as well, they will realize that memorizing material will not suffice. They must use various learning strategies and be active participants in the learning process to achieve the intended outcomes.

Instructional objectives also provide a basis for student self-assessment of learning progress. If students are to become independent learners, they must develop self-assessment skills. In writing, for example, students are required to review and revise their written work before submitting it. This requires a clear conception of the qualities of good writing. This can be done through well-stated writing objectives. Sharing with students the intended outcomes of a performance or skill at the beginning of the instruction provides not only direction to their learning but also a basis for evaluating their own progress and developing needed self-assessment and self-regulation skills.

Role of Objectives in Formative and Summative Assessment

Well-stated instructional objectives make clear the type of performance to be assessed. They describe what students should know and be able to do as a result of learning. Formative assessment is a matter of monitoring the process and products of student learning, and providing feedback about that particular type of performance. Summative assessment is then a matter of using an assessment instrument that best measures that particular type of performance. If it is a knowledge outcome, a paper-and-pencil test might do. But if it is a performance outcome (e.g., writing, speaking, psychomotor skill), some method of judging the performance skill or resulting product is required. Here the instructional objectives help clarify the criteria to be used in judging the performance and the type of assessment technique needed.

In addition to help in preparing assessment instruments, objectives also provide a basis for interpreting the results. When the assessment is keyed directly to the objectives, it is possible to describe what specific learning outcomes have been achieved and where review or remedial work is needed. For example, students may be able to define the basic terms of a unit but be unable to distinguish between those similar in meaning, or use the terms in a sentence. Similarly, students may be able to compute from a formula but be unable to solve a problem that requires use of the formula. Assessment instruments based on objectives make these types of interpretation possible.

Assessment is not limited to the end of instruction. It also can be used at the beginning of instruction to determine readiness for learning or the proper placement of students, and during instruction to guide student learning. For each of these uses it is important to have a clear statement of your intended learning outcomes so that instruction, student learning, and assessment are all working toward the same goals.

Role of Objectives in Communicating Instructional Intent to Others

We have already noted that clear instructional objectives communicate learning targets to students and, in so doing, support student participation in the learning process. In addition, instructional objectives that are stated as intended learning outcomes help clarify to parents, and others, how students will demonstrate that they have learned. Objectives also provide teachers with a basis for selecting samples of students' work to share with parents in parent-teacher conferences. Essentially, this process enables teachers to say, "This is what students are expected to achieve," and, "This is how well your child is doing it."

Role of Objectives in Evaluating Instruction

Clearly stated instructional objectives can help make clear the successes and failures in your instruction. This enables you to look for the reasons for failure in the methods, the materials, or the objectives themselves. In some cases you may need to change the methods and materials of instruction (e.g., use more complex material and student participation to develop reasoning skills). In others, you may need to modify the objectives or make them clearer to students.

Learning Outcomes and the Instructional Process

The relation of learning outcomes to the learning experiences provided during the teaching–learning phase of instruction is shown in Figure 1.4.

Figure 1.4 makes clear the fact that the learning experiences provided during the teaching–learning process are not ends in themselves but means to ends. The subject matter, the teaching methods, and the materials used in instruction are to be viewed as tools to bring about desired learning outcomes.

Although the diagram appears simple, the *process* of instruction and the *products* of instruction are frequently confused in statements of instructional objectives. For example, which of the following objectives is stated as a *product* (i.e., a learning *outcome*)?

1. Increases proficiency in the use of charts and graphs.
2. Interprets charts and graphs.

You are correct if you selected the second objective, which describes in general terms what the student does at the end of the learning experience. You later would want to clarify further what you mean by *interprets* (e.g., identifies a given point on a graph, describes the trend shown in a graph), but this instructional objective is definitely stated as a learning *product*.

In the first statement the term *increases* provides a clue that you are concerned with a *process*. The statement doesn't clarify how the student is to demonstrate increased proficiency at the end of the instruction. Is the student to interpret charts and graphs, to construct charts and graphs, or to give a speech in which charts and graphs will be used as visual aids? Stating objectives in terms of the learning *process* is misleading because one learning experience may contribute to many different learning outcomes, and one learning outcome (e.g., a scientific attitude) may be the result of many different learning experiences.

Figure 1.4   Relationship of Learning Outcomes and Learning Experiences

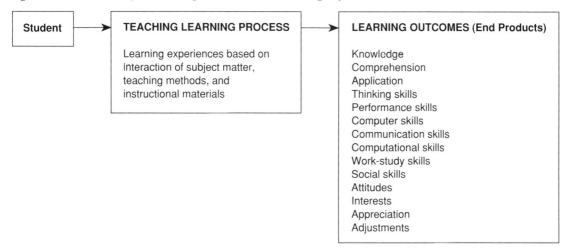

Stating Instructional Objectives as Intended Learning Outcomes

Instructional objectives can be stated as learning outcomes in two ways. One is to list each specific type of performance students are to exhibit at the end of the instructional period. For example, you might start a list concerned with terminology as follows:

1. Defines the term in their own words.
2. Identifies the meaning of the term when used in context.
3. Distinguishes among terms that are similar in meaning.

A second method is to state the general instructional objectives and then to clarify each objective by listing a *sample* of the specific types of student performance we are willing to accept as evidence of the attainment of that objective. This procedure would result in statements such as the following:

1. Comprehends the meaning of terms.
    1.1. Defines the term in their own words.
    1.2. Identifies the meaning of the term when used in context.
    1.3. Distinguishes among terms that are similar in meaning.

Note that the specific statements are the same in both instances. The first list, however, implies that these types of performance are ends in themselves and that instruction is to be given directly in the specified performance. For example, we teach students "to define a term in their own words," then, to test achievement of the outcome, we ask them "to define the term in their own words." This one-to-one relationship between the performance taught and the performance tested is characteristic of the training level and is widely used in programmed instruction. For regular classroom instruction, however, this procedure is useful only for teaching the simplest skills and the lowest levels of knowledge.

Stating the general instructional objective first and then clarifying it further by listing the specific types of performance that characterize that objective is more than a matter of literary form. This procedure makes clear that the instructional objective is *comprehension* and not *defining, identifying,* or *distinguishing among.* These latter terms simply describe a *sample of the types of performance that represent comprehension:* A different sample of specific types of performance could serve equally well. For example, you might use the following list instead of the one cited earlier.

1. Comprehends the meaning of terms.
    1.1. Relates terms to the concepts they represent.
    1.2. Uses each term in an original sentence.
    1.3. Identifies similarities and differences between terms.

Note that the instructional objective is still *comprehension.* We have merely listed a new sample of student performance to characterize what is meant by the statement "Comprehends the meaning of terms." It would be impossible to list all types of performance that might show comprehension; therefore, we must settle for a representative sample.

The particular sample of student performance you select to define an objective depends on both the level of the instruction and the nature of the content. The general objective "Comprehends the meaning of terms" could be an appropriate learning outcome at the elementary, secondary, or college level. However, at the elementary level the sample of performance might consist of specific statements such as "identifies pictures of the term" (e.g., largest) and "follows directions indicated by the term" (e.g., add these numbers), whereas at the high school or college level such specific outcomes as "describes the concept the term represents" and "uses the term correctly in stating a principle" may be more appropriate. Similarly, the specific sample of performance can vary somewhat with the subject being taught. For example, English teachers may find that statements such as "defines the term in their own words" and "uses the term in an original sentence" best clarify their intended outcomes, whereas science teachers may favor such statements as "distinguishes among terms" and "describes the process represented by the term." Thus, teachers at all levels and in various subject-matter areas might use some of the same general objectives, such as "Comprehends the meaning of terms," but each may describe the student performance they are willing to accept as evidence of comprehension differently, depending on the level and nature of the instruction. Thus, it is the list of specific statements that describes the intended learning outcomes in terms of student performance. These are called *specific learning outcomes* (see Figure 1.5).

The fact that specific learning outcomes simply serve as *samples* of the types of performance we are willing to accept as evidence of the attainment of our general instructional objectives has implications for both teaching and assessment. Our teaching efforts must be directed toward the general objectives of instruction and not toward the specific samples of performance we have selected to represent each objective. For example, in teaching a *comprehension of terms*, we might have the students study the textbook definitions, compare and contrast the terms during class discussion, and use the terms in oral and written work. When we test the students, however, we present them with a list of terms and

Figure 1.5   Some Basic Terminology

General Instructional Objective	An intended outcome of instruction that has been stated in general enough terms to encompass a domain of student performance (e.g., "Comprehends the literal meaning of written material"). A general instructional objective must be further defined by a set of specific learning outcomes to clarify instructional intent.
Specific Learning Outcome	An intended outcome of instruction that has been stated in terms of specific and observable *student performance* (e.g., "Identifies details that are explicitly stated in a passage"). Specific learning outcomes describe the types of performance that learners will be able to exhibit when they have achieved a general instructional objective (specific learning outcomes are also called *specific objectives, performance objectives,* and *measurable objectives*).
Student Performance	Any measurable or observable student response that is a result of learning.

ask them to define each term in their own words and to write an original sentence using the term. Note that the test calls for a type of response that was not directly taught during classroom instruction. This is necessary if the test results are to show a *comprehension* rather than merely a *recall* of previous learning. Also, the test calls forth only a sample of the types of performance that might be used to represent a *comprehension of terms*. It would be impractical to include test items that measure all aspects of understanding, just as it would be impractical to include all relevant terms in a particular test. In both cases we must be satisfied with a *sample*—a sample of the many terms that the students have studied during instruction and a sample of the many types of performance that could be used as evidence of the student's comprehension of terms. If our samples are carefully chosen, we can generalize from our test results to the larger achievement domain. That is, we can estimate how well the students have achieved our instructional objective, the *comprehension of terms*.

Although it is the specific learning outcomes that specify the types of learning responses we are willing to accept as evidence of learning, the statements of general objectives provide several useful functions:

1. They make clear the variety of types of learning expected from the instruction (i.e., knowledge, comprehension, thinking skills, performance skills).
2. They provide a focus for instruction that avoids concentrating on isolated and unrelated learning tasks.
3. They are general enough to permit flexibility in choosing teaching methods and materials.
4. They provide a framework for planning and preparing assessments and for interpreting assessment results.

What About Standards?

The method of stating objectives described here does not include the *standards* for determining a satisfactory level of performance. In a training program based on limited and specific tasks, it may be desirable to incorporate the required levels of performance in statements of the learning outcomes. For example, you might have statements like the following:

Keyboards 40 words per minute with no more than two errors per 40 words.

Locates an electronic malfunction in five minutes.

Sets up and tests equipment in 15 minutes.

Measures a length to the nearest sixteenth of an inch.

Where more complex learning outcomes are involved, it is desirable to state the standards separately so that there is no need to rewrite the objectives to fit different situations or different groups of learners. The current emphasis on holistic learning and problem solving in realistic contextual settings also calls for more general standards than those tied to each specific learning outcome. This approach typically requires describing standards of excellence in terms of a general procedure (e.g., planning a research study) or a general product (e.g., a written report). Assessment of the process or product uses holistic scoring rubrics (e.g., scoring guidelines) that describe levels of excellence for the process of the product as a whole. Thus, for complex learning outcomes, broader statements of standards are needed to reflect the integrated nature of the intended learning outcome.

There are two types of standards that are receiving widespread attention in education. There are *content standards* that describe what students should know and be able to do in a school subject and *performance standards* that describe the level of achievement that students are expected to attain.

Content standards have been developed by professional organizations and most states. Although the lists of content standards vary considerably, they typically emphasize complex learning outcomes such as understanding, thinking skills, and performance skills. It is assumed that schools will use the standards to fashion a curriculum that raises the level of learning for all students. Content standards provide a general framework for instructional planning, but instructional objectives are needed to convert the standards into measurable outcomes that can serve as targets for both teaching and assessment. Content standards are described and illustrated in Chapter 4.

Performance standards indicate how well the students should perform. Are they effective problem solvers? Do they demonstrate sound reasoning ability? Do they communicate effectively? These and similar questions indicate the problem of setting performance standards. We need some way to describe the level of performance that is to be attained. For want of a better system with complex learning outcomes, we have typically used criteria for effectiveness and arranged these in rating scales or holistic scoring rubrics to use in judging the students' level of performance. The criteria for effectiveness are typically derived from the instructional objectives. This procedure is described in Chapter 12.

Summary

1. Instructional objectives are most useful when stated as intended learning outcomes and defined in terms of student performance.

2. Objectives at the training level are typically stated as specific, limited, and well-defined tasks to be performed rather than goals to work toward. This provides for the modifying and shaping of student behavior to fit a predetermined set of responses. There is a one-to-one relationship between the teaching of the tasks and the testing of the tasks.

3. Objectives for higher-level learning outcomes (e.g., comprehension, problem solving, reasoning) focus on more complex and integrated patterns of response. The teaching and testing of specific learning tasks is replaced by greater emphasis on holistic learning and the assessment of more general response patterns. Objectives at this level provide goals to work toward, but the teacher is free to use a variety of methods and materials to help students achieve the intended learning outcomes.

4. When instructional objectives are stated as intended learning outcomes they provide direction for instruction, guidelines for student learning, targets for formative and summative assessment, a means to convey instructional intent to others, and a basis for the evaluation of instruction.

5. The two-step process of stating the general instructional objectives and further defining them with specific learning outcomes provides a focus for teaching, learning, and assessment without limiting the teacher's flexibility in selecting instructional methods and materials.

6. Although it may be possible to state all of the specific learning outcomes for some simple learning tasks (e.g., constructs a graph), for most classroom instruction only a sample of the specific outcomes can be stated for each objective.

7. The specific learning outcomes describe what types of student performance indicate that an objective has been achieved. Thus, common, general objectives (e.g., comprehends concepts) can be adapted to various content areas and levels of instruction by writing specific learning outcomes that are relevant to the particular situation.

8. Standards of performance may be included in statements of specific learning outcomes for a training program, but should not be included in the objectives used for classroom instruction. Writing standards separately removes the need to rewrite the objectives to fit different situations and different groups of learners. It also allows for the more general standards used with complex learning outcomes.

9. Both content standards and performance standards are receiving widespread attention in education. Content standards describe what students should learn and performance standards describe how well they should learn it. Instructional objectives play an important role in both. They describe the content standards in measurable terms and they provide criteria for describing the performance standards.

Exercises*

1. What does it mean to specify intended learning *outcomes* (as opposed to procedures, for example)? How does stating instructional objectives as intended learning outcomes help in planning and instruction?

2. Explain why it is a good thing to use both general instructional objectives and specific learning outcomes as part of your instructional objectives. What is the function of each, and how do they complement each other?

* *Note:* In the most straightforward sense, the reader will see that each specific learning outcome in a chapter could be rephrased as an exercise, for example: "Describe . . ." "Distinguish . . ." "Explain . . ." and so on. We encourage readers to self-assess in this manner. In the interest of conserving space and time, the exercises for each chapter use a subset of its specific learning outcomes. We have selected some of the more basic outcomes. Appendix F presents suggested answers to the exercises.

Chapter 2

Obtaining Clear Statements of Instructional Objectives

INSTRUCTIONAL OBJECTIVE:

Writes clear statements of general instructional objectives and specific learning outcomes.

1. Distinguishes between well-stated and poorly stated general instructional objectives.
2. Describes the procedure for defining general instructional objectives in performance terms.
3. Distinguishes among verbs that indicate instructional intent and those that are merely learning indicators.
4. Writes a set of instructional objectives for a unit or course of instruction.
5. Prepares a list of criteria for determining whether a set of instructional objectives is well stated.

As we explained in the first chapter, objectives for most classroom learning should be stated in two steps: (1) stating the general instructional objectives as intended learning outcomes, and (2) defining each general instructional objective by listing a sample of the specific types of student performance that represent achievement of the objectives. The procedure sounds simple enough, but many teachers find it difficult at first. Here we describe and illustrate how to state instructional objectives that clearly convey instructional intent and provide an effective guide for teaching, learning, and assessment.

Stating the General Instructional Objectives

To help you clearly state general instructional objectives as intended learning outcomes, perhaps the easiest place to start is with what *not* to do. One of the most common errors, mentioned earlier, is to describe teacher performance rather than student performance.

Look at the following two objectives, for example, and note the difference in how they are stated. Which one most clearly indicates an instructional outcome?

1. Comprehends assigned reading material.
2. To increase the students' reading ability.

You should have had little difficulty selecting the first statement, which contains an expected outcome of instruction. Later we would need to list a sample of the specific types of performance that we are willing to accept as evidence that the student *comprehends*, but as stated this is a good general outcome.

The second statement offers a less clear picture of the intended results of instruction. It also gives the psychologically unsound impression that it is the teacher who is going to do the increasing rather than the student.

Another common error was also mentioned in Chapter 1; that is, stating an objective in terms of the learning *process* rather than as a learning *product*. The following two statements will clarify the difference. Which one is stated as a *product* of instruction, i.e., an instructional *outcome*?

1. Gains knowledge of basic principles.
2. Applies basic principles to new situations.

If you selected the second statement, you are correct. This statement clearly indicates what the student can do at the end of instruction. The first statement emphasizes the *gaining* of knowledge—the learning *process* rather than the type of performance that provides evidence that learning has taken place. Words like *gains, acquires,* and *develops* give away the fact that an objective is focused on the learning *process* rather than on the expected *outcome* of the learning experience.

In some cases in which objectives are stated in terms of the learning process, the instructional intent is still fairly clear. This is often true for simple learning outcomes. For example, in the statement "Develops skill in adding whole numbers," the learning outcome is obvious. In other cases, however, a single learning experience might contribute to any number of learning outcomes, none of which is apparent in the statement of objectives. For example, look at the following statement:

Learns symbols on a weather map.

This statement does clarify what the student is to learn, but it does not clarify the learning *outcomes* toward which the student should be directed. The teacher who wrote this statement might have in mind any one of the following learning outcomes:

Recalls the symbols used on a weather map.

Identifies the symbols on a weather map.

Interprets a weather map (using the symbols).

Constructs a weather map (using the symbols).

Predicts weather from a weather map (using the symbols).

The statement "learns symbols" obviously does not indicate the intent of the instruction as clearly as the statements of learning *outcomes* in the list. Identifying the nature of the desired product provides greater direction for planning, carrying out, and assessing the learning experiences.

Another common error in stating objectives is simply to list the subject matter to be covered. This error can be seen in a comparison of the following two statements. Which one is properly stated?

1. Principles of electricity.

2. Comprehends basic principles.

The correct answer is, of course, the second statement. The first statement is no more than a subject-matter topic. It contains no indication of what the students are expected to do with regard to the principles of electricity. Are they simply to know them, to comprehend them, or to apply them in some way?

The second statement could read "Comprehends principles of electricity," but there is some advantage in broadening the statement to include all types of principles covered in the instruction. The same outcome can then be used to indicate the expected reaction to any principle studied. When this is done, the specific types of student response used to clarify what is meant by the word *comprehends* must, of course, be *performance* oriented rather than *content* oriented. When complete, the statement of the objective and of the specific learning *outcomes* might appear as follows:

1. Comprehends basic principles.
    1.1. States the principle in his or her own words.
    1.2. Identifies an example of the principle.
    1.3. Distinguishes between correct and incorrect applications of the principle.
    1.4. Predicts an outcome based on the principle.

Note that the specific statements do not indicate what principles the students are to comprehend, but rather what *performance* they are to demonstrate as evidence that they comprehend. By not including a reference to subject matter in statements of learning outcomes, you can develop a set of outcomes that is useful with various units of instruction throughout a course. Thus the subject matter in each unit of instruction will indicate the principles that are to be studied, and the learning *outcomes* will indicate the types of reactions the students are to make to the principles.

Another common error is to include more than one type of learning *outcome* in each general objective. Look at the following two statements. Which one contains a *single outcome*?

1. Uses appropriate experimental procedures in solving problems.

2. Knows the scientific method and applies it effectively.

The first statement is correct; the second statement includes both *knows* and *applies* as possible *outcomes*. It is better to have a separate statement for each because some students

Figure 2.1   Stating Instructional Objectives

Observe the following precautions when stating instructional objectives:

1. Don't state them in terms of *teacher performance*. (e.g., "Teach students scientific concepts.")
2. Don't state them in terms of the *learning* process. (e.g., "Student learns scientific concepts.")
3. Don't focus on the *subject-matter* topics. (e.g., "Student learns the meaning of osmosis, photosynthesis, etc.")
4. Don't include two objectives in one statement. (e.g., "Student knows and comprehends scientific concepts.")

State and define each objective in terms of the type of *student performance* that is to be demonstrated at the end of instruction, as illustrated below:

1. Comprehends scientific concepts.
    1.1. Defines the concept.
    1.2. Identifies an example of the concept.
    1.3. States hypotheses based on the concept.
    1.4. Describes how the process functions in a given situation.
    1.5. Describes an experiment that illustrates the process.

may know the scientific method (i.e., be able to describe it) but may not be able to apply it effectively. With separate statements, you can define each objective in terms of specific learning outcomes and thus determine how well each objective is being achieved.

In this section we have focused on some common errors to avoid in stating the general instructional objectives: stating the objectives in terms of (1) the teacher's performance, (2) the learning process, (3) the subject matter, and (4) a combination of two or more outcomes. These errors can be avoided by *focusing attention on the students and on the type of performance they are expected to demonstrate at the end of instruction*. Instructional objectives, then, should be brief, clear statements that describe instructional intent in terms of the desired learning *outcomes* (see Figure 2.1).

In addition to avoiding the common errors in stating instructional objectives, one of the most difficult tasks is to select the proper level of generality in stating each major objective.

Selecting the Proper Level of Generality

When developing a list of general instructional objectives for a course (or unit of course work), our aim is to create a list of outcomes to work toward and not a list of specific tasks to be performed by all students. To be sure, each general instructional objective will need to be defined further by a sample of the specific types of student performance that

Figure 2.2   Examples of General Instructional Objectives

Reading
1. Knows word meanings.
2. Comprehends the literal meaning of written material.
3. Infers meaning from written material.
4. Interprets tables, graphs, maps, and diagrams.
5. Evaluates written material using specific criteria (e.g., realistic, accurate).
6. Adapts reading rate to material and purpose of reading.
7. Locates information by using guides (e.g., index, table of contents, reference works).
8. Demonstrates a positive attitude toward reading.

Mathematics
1. Knows the meanings of terms and symbols.
2. Computes accurately and rapidly.
3. Comprehends mathematical concepts and processes.
4. Comprehends the number systems.
5. Applies concepts and processes to mathematical problems.
6. Invents new mathematical applications or generalizations.
7. Interprets measuring instruments, tables, and graphs.
8. Demonstrates a positive attitude toward mathematics.

Science
1. Knows the meaning of terms.
2. Knows specific facts.
3. Knows laboratory procedures.
4. Comprehends concepts and principles.
5. Applies concepts and principles to new situations.
6. Demonstrates skills and abilities needed to conduct an experiment.
7. Interprets data in scientific reports.
8. Displays a scientific attitude.

characterize each objective, but at this stage we are focusing only on the stating of the general objectives (see Figure 2.2).

You may have noticed by now that each of the instructional objectives used in this chapter to illustrate properly stated learning outcomes began with a verb. The following verbs were used in these statements:

applies

comprehends

knows

uses

These verbs provide a clue to the desired level of generality for our major objectives. They are specific enough to provide direction for instruction without overly restricting the teacher or reducing the instruction to the training level. They are also specific enough to be easily defined by a brief list of the types of performance students are to demonstrate when the objectives have been achieved.

Let's look at a few statements that illustrate the problem of selecting a proper level of generality. Which one of the following statements represents the most general objective? Which one the most specific?

1. Communicates effectively in English.
2. Writes clear, effective English.
3. Punctuates sentences properly.

The first statement represents the most general objective. In fact, it is probably too general for a major objective because communication includes speaking, listening, writing, and reading. Each of these areas is general enough to provide a major objective by itself.

The most specific is the third statement, which might be a good specific learning outcome to be listed under a more general objective, but is probably too specific to be used as a general instructional objective. Thus the second statement comes closest to the desired level of generality. It clearly indicates the nature of the expected learning *outcome*, and it can be defined by a relatively short, clear list of specific learning outcomes.

Stating the Specific Learning Outcomes

After preparing a tentative list of general instructional objectives, you are ready to define each general objective in terms of the specific types of student performance that you are willing to accept as evidence that the objective has been achieved. These *specific learning outcomes* provide an operational definition of what we mean when we state that a student "knows terms," "comprehends principles," or "interprets charts and graphs." Unless the general objectives are further clarified in this way, they will not provide an adequate framework for teaching, student learning, or assessment.

The following general instructional objective and list of specific learning outcomes illustrates what is meant by defining instructional objectives in terms of *student performance*.

1. Knows specific facts (U.S. history).
    1.1. Identifies important dates, events, places, and people.
    1.2. Describes the characteristics of a given historical period.
    1.3. Lists important events in chronological order.
    1.4. Relates events to their most probable causes.

Note that each specific learning outcome starts with an *action verb* that indicates *observable* student responses; that is, responses that can be seen by an outside observer. These verbs are listed as follows to clarify the types of terms needed for stating the specific learning outcomes:

identifies

describes

lists

relates

These verbs describe the types of responses the students are to exhibit as evidence that they have achieved the general instructional objective "Knows specific facts." As noted earlier, these responses provide only a sample of the specific outcomes that could be included under this objective. The list might be lengthened, shortened, or radically modified to fit the emphasis of a particular course. As a teacher you must define your own instructional objectives in terms of the specific learning outcomes you deem most appropriate. All we are doing here is illustrating the process of stating the specific outcomes in terms of identifiable student performance.

To check on your ability to distinguish between appropriate and inappropriate terms, look at the following two statements. Which one is stated in terms of student performance?

1. Realizes the importance of neatness.
2. Explains the importance of neatness.

You are correct if you selected the second statement. The term "explains" indicates a response that is definite and observable. The first statement does not specify how students will demonstrate that they *realize* the importance of neatness. Will they give reasons for being neat or will they dress more neatly? Terms such as this are subject to many interpretations and should be avoided when you state the specific learning outcomes for each general objective. Let's try another pair of statements to be sure you can tell the difference between *performance* and *nonperformance* terms. Which one of the following clearly indicates student performance?

1. Predicts the outcome of an experiment.
2. Sees the value of an experiment.

This time you should have had little difficulty in selecting the first statement as the correct answer. The term "sees" in the second statement is a common one in education (e.g., "I see the point"), and its familiarity might have misled you. But *sees* refers to an internal state. What will the students do when they see the value of an experiment? Will they describe its usefulness, point out its theoretical implications, or estimate the social consequences of the results? We simply can't tell because the term *sees* is vague, indefinite, and describes a reaction that is not directly observable.

In stating specific learning outcomes, then, it is wise to begin each statement with a verb that specifies definite, observable student performance. Such statements clarify from the outset the types of responses students are expected to make when they have achieved the general objective. Helpful lists of verbs for stating specific learning outcomes are included in Appendix E.

Although some verbs in Appendix E seem rather elementary, don't be hesitant to use them if they clearly indicate the desired student performance. Take the verb "draw," for example. This word is typically associated with learning outcomes at the elementary level, where verbal ability is limited. Thus, we may ask students to draw a circle or square to see if they are learning these basic concepts. At higher levels of education, however, we may ask students to draw a weather map, an electronic circuit, or a floor plan for a house. Thus, the verb simply indicates the nature of the performance and not the difficulty of the learning outcome. What follows the verb typically determines the complexity and difficulty of the performance to be demonstrated.

Obtaining a Representative Sample of Specific Learning Outcomes

When you define a general objective with a list of specific learning outcomes, you will need to decide how many specific outcomes to list for each objective. No hard-and-fast rules exist for this. Simple knowledge and skill outcomes obviously will require fewer specific outcomes than more complex ones, but even relatively simple instructional objectives may encompass such a large number of specific types of performance that only a portion of them can be listed. Take "knowledge of terms," for example, and note the various types of student performance that might be listed.

1. Knows the meaning of terms.
    1.1. Writes a definition of the term.
    1.2. Identifies a definition of the term.
    1.3. Identifies the term that fits a given description.
    1.4. Identifies a synonym of the term.
    1.5. Identifies an antonym of the term.
    1.6. Identifies an example of the term.
    1.7. Identifies the term represented by a symbol (e.g., +, −).
    1.8. Draws a picture that represents the term (e.g., circle, square).
    1.9. Describes the procedure the term represents.
    1.10. States the concept or principle that fits the term.
    1.11. Describes the relationship of the term to a second term.
    1.12. Differentiates between the term and a second term.
    1.13. Differentiates between the technical meaning and the common meaning of the term.
    1.14. Identifies the best meaning of the term when used in a sentence.
    1.15. Distinguishes between proper and improper usage of the term.

This list is not exhaustive, making clear the futility of attempting to list all possible specific types of responses that represent a particular objective. All we can reasonably expect to do is list a sample of the specific types of performance that the students are expected to demonstrate when they have achieved the objective. The aim is to select as representative a sample as possible, so that students' performance on the selected outcomes will be characteristic of what their performance would be like on similar outcomes encompassed by the same general instructional objective. Typically, four to eight specific learning outcomes will be sufficient to describe an objective, but in some cases (e.g., a complex learning outcome) more outcomes may be needed.

The specific outcomes that best represent a general instructional objective will be modified by both the nature of the subject taught and the grade level at which the instruction is given. For "knowing terms," for example, a reading teacher would be likely to stress the identification of synonyms, antonyms, the meaning of words in context, and similar outcomes related to reading ability, whereas a math teacher would emphasize outcomes that relate the meaning of terms to symbols (e.g., $\times$, $=$), figures (e.g., types of angles), operations (e.g., grouping into *sets*), and the like. Similarly, a primary teacher would be likely to state fewer and simpler types of outcomes based on picture identification and student drawings.

When the instructional objectives are *complex*, special care is needed to include all key elements. To identify the key elements in complex objectives, it is often necessary to consult reference books and other relevant materials. You are not likely to find a neat list of outcomes from which to choose, but even general discussions of the concepts will help to define the objectives. Thus, when objectives are concerned with *thinking skills*, *scientific inquiry*, and the like, a trip to the library might be needed to determine the specific learning *outcomes* involved.

Complex objectives are difficult to define but are usually more important from an educational standpoint. Don't overload your list of instructional objectives with simple learning outcomes merely because they are easy to define.

Emphasizing Instructional Intent

The *action verb* is the key element in stating the specific learning outcomes that define each general instructional objective. The selection of action verbs thus is a vital step in the preparation of a useful set of objectives. In general, select those verbs that (1) most clearly convey your instructional intent and (2) most precisely specify the student performance you are willing to accept as evidence that the general instructional objective has been achieved. Unfortunately, action verbs vary widely in their ability to meet both criteria.

Some verbs communicate instructional intent well but are less precise concerning the specific response to be observed. Other verbs clearly indicate the performance to be observed, but the indicated response does not satisfactorily convey the intent of the instruction. Let's look at a few examples. Which one of the following most clearly conveys instructional intent? Which one most precisely specifies the performance to be observed?

1. Identifies the parts on a diagram for an electrical circuit.
2. Labels the parts on a diagram for an electrical circuit.

If you selected the first statement as most clearly conveying instructional intent, you are correct. In this particular instance, the focus of our instruction would be on the *identification* of the parts and not the labeling of them. Although the term *labels* is more descriptive of the precise response the students are expected to make, labeling is not the intended learning outcome. We assume students already know how to label.

In this instance, we are simply using labeling as one way that identification might be shown. Identification might also be shown by pointing to, touching, drawing, circling, underlining, and so on. These *indicators* of the "ability to identify" clearly specify the student performance, but they do not always make clear the *intent* of the instruction. Given a choice between the two, it is wise to select the verb that best conveys instructional intent when stating specific learning outcomes.

Keeping the Specific Learning Outcomes Useful for Various Units of Study

The specific learning outcomes need to be specific enough to convey instructional intent but general enough to be used with various units of study. For example, the following statements represent specific learning tasks for a particular lesson:

1. Identifies the parts of the heart.
2. Describes the functions of the heart.

These specific tasks can best be converted into more general statements of specific learning outcomes as follows:

1. Identifies the parts of a given structure.
2. Describes the functions of a given structure.

Statements like these clearly describe what type of performance the students are to demonstrate, but the responses are not tied to a specific body part. In fact, the revised statements would be useful with any animal or plant structure being studied. The advantage of keeping the statements broader is, of course, that a set of objectives can then be used with various units of study. The subject-matter topics in each unit specify the content the student is to react to, and the specific learning outcomes describe the types of reactions to be made by the students.

To be sure you grasp this distinction, look at the following pair of learning outcomes and decide which one would be most useful with various units of study:

1. Lists the major battles of World War II in chronological order.
2. Lists historical events in chronological order.

The second one is a common learning outcome that can be used repeatedly in a history course. This statement also illustrates that sometimes all you need to do is substitute generalized content (e.g., historical events) for specific content (e.g., World War II). Thus, when you find yourself listing specific tasks such as the following, you might simply combine them into a single statement like "Distinguishes among geometric shapes."

1. Distinguishes between a circle and a square.
2. Distinguishes between a square and a rectangle.
3. Distinguishes between a rectangle and a triangle.

There is nothing basically wrong with combining the student responses and specific course content. This approach is useful for brief units of work and is especially helpful to beginning teachers when planning lessons. Even here, however, it is better to define the objectives for a course of instruction in more general terms and use the statements as models or templates for stating the tasks for specific lessons.

Using Specific Learning Outcomes in Lesson Planning

We have been describing how to state specific learning outcomes so they will be useful with various units of study. When planning specific lessons you will, of course, want to combine the specific learning outcomes with the course content to indicate precisely what students can do to demonstrate achievement. Thus, the generalized statements can be used as models or templates in identifying and stating the specific learning outcomes of a lesson. For example, statements like "Identifies the parts of a given structure" and "Identifies the functions of a given structure" provide guidelines that can be repeatedly used in different lessons where they are combined with the content, as follows:

Identifies the parts of a flower.

Describes the function of each flower part.

Identifies the parts of the circulatory system.

Describes the function of each part of the circulatory system.

Identifies the parts of the microscope.

Describes the function of each part of the microscope.

These types of statements are especially useful to new teachers when planning for instruction and assessment. Experienced teachers, however, find it easier to make the transition to specific lessons without rewriting the intended outcome to fit the specific content. Thus, whether they are teaching about animals, plants, or laboratory equipment, they expect students to identify the parts and describe the functions of any structure studied.

The value of generalized statements of specific learning outcomes is not limited to simple learning outcomes. In describing reasoning ability in a specific content domain, for example, a statement such as "Describes the similarities and differences between two things" can be applied to plants, animals, objects, processes, laws, and anything else one wishes to have compared. Thus, they serve as a guide for more content-oriented statements. In science, for example, it might be "Describes the similarities and differences between plant and animal cells." In social studies, it might be "Describes the similarities and differences between the Democratic and Republican parties." In any event, the generalized statements provide models or templates for the more content-oriented statements used in lesson planning.

Making Sure the Specific Learning Outcomes are Relevant

It goes without saying that each specific learning outcome should be relevant to the instructional objective it is defining, but this criterion constitutes another area of difficulty in listing the specific statements. Look at the following two statements, for example. Which one should be listed under the general goal "comprehends scientific principles"?

1. Makes a prediction using the principle.
2. States the textbook definition of the principle.

Given a choice between these two, we would have to select the first. The second statement implies no more than the simple recall of information and therefore would be best classified as a *knowledge* outcome. The first statement goes beyond the recall of previously learned facts and asks the student to use the principle in a way that reflects a comprehension of its meaning.

Revising the General Objectives as Needed

During the process of defining the general instructional objectives, it may be necessary to modify the original list. In identifying the specific learning outcomes for the objectives, you may realize that some of them are too general and need to be subdivided. An objective on *problem solving* in arithmetic, for example, might better express instructional intent if it is broken down into *computational skill* and *solving story problems*. In defining other objectives, you might note that the specific learning outcomes overlap to such a degree that it is desirable to combine two statements into a single objective. Thus, "applies scientific procedures" and "plans simple experiments" might best be combined into a single objective such as "uses the scientific method effectively." Because instructional objectives can be stated in many ways and at various levels of generality, considerable flexibility exists in the formulation of the statements. The listing of the specific learning outcomes thus provides a good opportunity for evaluating the original list of instructional objectives and for revising them as necessary. The ultimate aim, of course, is to derive a final list of general objectives and specific learning outcomes that most clearly indicates your instructional intent. Use the checklist in Appendix A for evaluating your final list of objectives.

Summary

1. State each general instructional objective as an *intended learning outcome* (i.e., in terms of students' terminal performance).
2. Begin each general objective with a verb that encompasses a domain of student performance (e.g., *knows, comprehends, applies*). Omit "The student is able to. . . ."
3. State each general objective so that it includes only one general learning outcome (e.g., not "Knows and comprehends. . . .").

4. State each general objective in a manner that is useful with various units of study (e.g., "Knows the meaning of terms.").

5. State each general objective so that it encompasses a readily definable domain of specific learning outcomes and is free from overlapping with other objectives.

6. List beneath each general instructional objective a set of specific learning outcomes that indicates the types of terminal performance the students can demonstrate when they have achieved the objective.

7. Begin each specific learning outcome with an action verb that specifies *observable performances* and indicates *instructional intent* (e.g., *identifies, describes*).

8. The set of specific learning outcomes for each instructional objective should be relevant, representative, and useful with various units of study.

9. Use the specific learning outcomes as models or templates when combining them with specific content in lesson planning.

10. When defining the general instructional objectives in terms of specific learning outcomes, revise and refine the original list of general objectives as needed.

11. Don't neglect complex objectives (e.g., thinking skills) simply because they are difficult to define in terms of specific learning outcomes. Consult reference materials for help.

12. Check your final list of learning outcomes to be sure it clearly conveys your instructional intent.

Exercises

1. In each pair of general instructional objectives that follows, identify which is better. Then tell why.

    a. Applies rounding rules.

       Learns how to round.

    b. Comprehends the plot of a novel.

       Reads a novel with understanding.

2. In each pair of specific learning outcomes that follows, identify which is better. Then tell why.

    a. Predicts the outcome of an experiment.

       Does an experiment with a lab partner.

    b. States the textbook definition of a principle.

       Applies a principle to solve problems.

Chapter 3

Using Objectives in Planning for Teaching and Assessment

INSTRUCTIONAL OBJECTIVE:

Uses instructional objectives in planning for teaching and assessment.

1. Describes how objectives can be used in instructional planning.
2. Prepares an instructional planning chart for a unit of instruction.
3. Describes the role of objectives in planning for assessment procedures.
4. Describes the various ways assessment procedures can be used in instruction.
5. Describes how sharing instructional objectives and assessment procedures with students can contribute to improved student learning.
6. Explains why it is important to write instructional objectives before selecting the teaching and assessment procedures.

Instructional objectives describe the types of performance students are expected to demonstrate as evidence of achievement. Thus, they should be prepared before you plan instructional strategies and design assessment methods. The proper sequence in instructional planning should be as follows:

1. Prepare the instructional objectives.
2. Select the methods and materials for instruction.
3. Design the assessment instruments.

Following these steps makes it possible to relate the classroom activities and assessment procedures directly to the intended learning outcomes.

Planning for Instruction

One way to ensure that the instructional objectives, the teaching, and the assessment procedures are in close harmony is to prepare a planning chart that includes all three. A simple example of a planning chart for teaching addition and subtraction at the early elementary level is presented in Table 3.1.

At this early level of work in math the instructional objectives, teaching, and assessment are hardly distinguishable from one another. They all deal with the basic math skills, but the emphasis is on the comprehension of the concepts of addition and subtraction. As students progress in the math program, you will expect them to be able to add, subtract, multiply, and divide at an automatic level. However, it is important that they comprehend the meaning of the concepts, as they will need this understanding later to solve more complex problems involving math. The instructional planning chart helps you focus on conceptual understanding in both the teaching and the assessment.

A second example of an instructional planning chart is shown in Table 3.2. This chart makes clear that objectives, teaching, and assessment are not on a one-to-one basis. The

Table 3.1   Instructional Planning Chart (Elementary Math)

Instructional Objectives	Teaching Methods	Assessment Procedures
Comprehends addition and subtraction concepts. 1. Explains concepts as "add on" or "take away" procedures. 2. Demonstrates use of concepts with objects (e.g., marbles). 3. Demonstrates use of concepts with pictures. 4. Relates the concepts to symbols (+, −, =). 5. Writes simple equations using the concepts.	Check to be sure all students have mastered counting. Start with concrete objects to explain the "add on" and "take away" procedures. Proceed to pictures and then to equation writing. Emphasize the inverse relationship between addition and subtraction. Give numerous examples and practice problems. Give feedback on practice problems.	Have students demonstrate the procedures with realistic problems and explain the procedures involved.
Solves story problems. 1. Selects the appropriate process (addition or subtraction). 2. Puts the problem in equation form. 3. Solves the problem. 4. Checks answer by using reverse procedure.	Describe and illustrate the steps in solving story problems emphasizing what is given, what is asked for, and how to convert to equation form and solve. Give numerous examples and practice problems. Allow students to explain their reasoning, diagram, or draw it. Give feedback on practice problems, on both the solution and the strategy used.	Story problems that require equation writing, solving, and checking with reverse procedure.

Table 3.2   Instructional Planning Chart (English)

Instructional Objectives	Teaching Methods	Assessment Procedures
Knows literary terms. 1. Writes textbook definitions. 2. Identifies examples in a literary selection. 3. Uses the terms correctly in oral and written work.	Encourage students to make a "literary dictionary," and to review the definitions periodically. Point out, and ask students to point out, examples during oral reading. Give oral and written assignments requiring use of the terms.	1. Short-answer test 2. Multiple-choice test 3. Observation and evaluation of written work
Interprets literary works. 1. Identifies the major and minor themes. 2. States the author's purpose or message. 3. Identifies the tone and mood. 4. Explains why the characters behave as they do. 5. Points out specific parts of the literature that support the above interpretations. 6. Relates the literary work to other writings.	Read a brief literary work to class. Lead off discussion with questions concerning theme, author's purpose, tone, and character development. Analyze the parts of the literary work and show how they support the general interpretations. Generalize the method of analysis and interpretation by applying it to a second work. Have students select a literary work and write a critical analysis and interpretation. Use teacher and peer feedback to improve the interpretation.	Observation during class discussions. Objective test on specific points in a literary work and on the process of literary analysis. Essay questions calling for interpretations and supporting evidence. Evaluation of student's written reports (using criteria of effective interpretation).

objectives indicate what you expect students to be able to do at the end of instruction, but the teaching method is simply suggestive of one way to do it. The assessment procedures are related to the teaching, but with different teaching procedures the assessment procedures may need to be modified. What you are striving for is a close match between goals, teaching, and assessment, and the chart helps you achieve that.

Although the instructional planning chart provides an overall plan for teaching, it is important to keep in mind that in classroom instruction you typically work on several learning outcomes at the same time. When focusing on "Interprets literary works," for example, you are also concerned with speaking skills, writing skills, and appreciation of literature. These would be spelled out separately in the planning chart, but the instruction would incorporate all of them. The daily lesson plans provide a place for this integration of learning experiences.

The same type of instructional planning that is illustrated in Tables 3.1 and 3.2 must, of course, be done for all intended learning outcomes for a given course of instruction. Most of the objectives will focus on particular areas of content, but some will focus on outcomes that are involved in all areas of content. For example, if reasoning ability is listed as an important outcome, it may be listed separately or may be included in the specific learning outcomes of relevant content areas. In any event, teaching methods and assessment procedures must reflect this emphasis on reasoning ability.

Planning for Assessment

Once you have prepared the instructional objectives, plan teaching procedures and then assessment. Sometimes you can plan instruction and assessment at the same time. Plan not only how to assess the intended outcomes but also when to prepare the instruments and where to use them. All too frequently teachers wait until the instruction is over, or nearly over, and then begin to prepare the assessment instruments. This limits the opportunity to use assessment to improve learning—which should be its main function. When assessment is viewed as part of the teaching–learning process, the plans for assessment are made before instruction starts. This might include preassessment of needed skills to begin instruction, assessment during instruction to determine learning progress and diagnose learning problems, and end of instruction assessment to determine final mastery of intended learning outcomes.

Assessment Before Instruction

Before instruction begins it is important to determine if students have the prerequisite knowledge and skills needed to successfully achieve the intended learning outcomes. This may be as simple as checking to make sure students can count before learning addition or subtraction, as noted in Table 3.1 under Teaching Methods. In other cases, a comprehensive test that covers the necessary knowledge and skills may be required. When beginning an algebra course, for example, a test of arithmetic and other required skills will help determine the readiness of students to learn algebra. Similarly, a test of English grammar may be useful preceding the study of a foreign language. In any area of instruction that has clearly defined prerequisites, a readiness test is desirable.

In some cases, a test of the intended learning outcomes of the instruction may be desirable. If students have already mastered the material to be taught, they can be placed at a higher level of instruction. If only some of the objectives have been achieved, you can adjust the intended learning outcomes and instruction to fit the students' achievement background. Where individualized instruction is used, the pretest can help determine the best starting point for each student.

Whether preassessment is necessary depends to a large extent on the nature of the instruction. In an area like mathematics, which is highly structured and each level of achievement requires mastery of earlier learning, preassessment of content knowledge is very important. In less structured areas, more important areas for preassessment may be prior experiences with the topic, attitudes, and interest.

Assessment During Instruction

Students are most likely to be successful when you use formative assessment to monitor student progress toward achievement of the objectives. Some of this assessment will, of course, be your daily observation during instruction and student self-assessment as they regulate their own studying. However, there is also a need for periodic testing, practice exercises, ratings of performance, and the like, to provide feedback to students concerning their learning progress and to provide remediation where needed. In formative assessment during instruction, teaching and assessment blend together in improving student learning. In addition to helping students directly, monitoring learning progress can also help you make adjustments in instruction. It can help you determine whether to move faster or slower, to review certain materials, to bring in instructional aids, or to modify students' assignments.

Assessment at the End of Instruction

Here we are interested in determining how well the students have achieved the intended learning outcomes of the instruction. Assessment at this point is used primarily for summative purposes like the assignment of grades or the certification of mastery. The results are still useful, however, for modifying future plans for instruction. If most students have difficulty with the application of knowledge or skills, for example, it may be necessary to modify the objectives, the teaching, or the assessment procedures. In any event, final assessment should be reviewed for any possible clues for improving instruction in the future.

Preparing and Using Assessment Procedures

Instructional objectives play a key role in the preparation of assessment procedures. The intended learning outcomes, specified by the objectives, clarify the types of student performance you are willing to accept as evidence of achievement. The assessment procedures provide a means of collecting that evidence. For example, if the learning outcomes are testable, we construct test items that call for the specific performance described in the intended outcome. Thus, "defines the basic terms of the unit" is tested by questions like "What is the definition of . . . ?" A specific learning outcome like "Identifies the proper application of . . ." can be tested by "Which of the following best illustrates the proper application of . . . ?" followed by several answers in multiple-choice form.

If the intended learning outcomes are clearly stated, there is no problem in constructing a valid test. Just match the test item to the learning outcome to be measured. The process of using objectives in test construction will be described and illustrated in a later chapter. Here we are simply emphasizing the important role of objectives in planning for the construction of tests.

When our intended learning outcomes are concerned with writing projects, problem-solving projects, and similar performance activities, we are required to seek other types of assessment procedures. In determining whether students can write, we ask them to write something. The writing is then assessed by the criteria used to judge good writing (e.g., well organized). When the objectives and specific learning outcomes are well stated, they provide the criteria for the assessment. Then all we need to do is use the statements in a rating scale, checklist, or some type of holistic scoring rubric (scoring guide). Here again, we are simply stressing the importance of objectives in preparing procedures for performance assessment. Later chapters will describe and illustrate the process in detail.

Although it would be difficult to prepare all assessment procedures before instruction begins, plans for their construction and use should be made before instruction. Share both your instructional objectives and plans for assessment with students at the beginning of instruction. This might include sample test items, descriptions of performance assessments, and how you will use the assessment procedures to improve learning. This will provide students with a guide for learning by making explicit the relationship between the learning activities, the intended learning outcomes, and the assessment procedures. Providing students with sample test items, like those used in the test, before testing and giving them copies of the scoring guides (e.g., rating forms) before engaging in the performance activities can also contribute to more effective learning. It gives the students clear achievement targets, provides a basis for assessing their own learning progress, and contributes to the development of independent learning—a major goal of education.

In planning for instruction and assessment, your goal should be how to design an instructional program that is most effective in improving student learning. This involves well-stated instructional objectives, well-designed teaching plans, effective assessment procedures, monitoring of learning progress, providing timely feedback to students, encouraging students to develop self-assessment skills, and moving students along toward self-direction and independent learning. It all begins with clearly stated intended learning outcomes. You have to know where you are going before you plan the trip.

Summary

1. Instructional objectives should be prepared before selecting the methods and materials of instruction and the assessment procedures. This makes it possible to relate the teaching procedures and assessment techniques directly to the intended learning outcomes.

2. One way of ensuring that the instructional objectives, the teaching, and the assessment procedures are in close harmony is to use a planning chart that includes all three.

3. The planning chart lists the objectives and specific learning outcomes in the first column, the teaching methods in the second column, and the assessment procedures in the third column. This chart states what the instruction is to achieve, how you plan to achieve it, and how you will determine the success of your instruction.

4. Assessment procedures are useful before instruction to determine student readiness or correct placement in the instruction, during instruction to monitor learning and provide feedback to students, and at the end of instruction to assign grades or certify mastery.

5. Planning for assessment should be made at the same time as the other plans for instruction, with emphasis on using the assessment procedures to improve student learning.

6. Sharing the instructional objectives and assessment procedures with students can provide clear targets for learning and contribute to self-assessment skills and independent learning.

7. Your goal in instructional planning is to determine what you expect students to achieve (objectives), how you plan to help them achieve it (teaching methods, including formative assessment), and what types of evidence you are willing to accept as evidence of achievement (summative assessment procedures). Effective instruction requires a close match between all three.

Exercises

1. Describe how you can use instructional objectives
   a. in planning for instruction.
   b. in planning for formative assessment.
   c. in planning for summative assessment.
   d. for sharing with students.

2. Consider the following objective. Explain how you would use it to plan instruction, inform instruction and student learning, and evaluate learning.
   A. Writes an effective persuasive essay.
   A.1. Clearly states main argument.
   A.2. Brings logic to bear on main argument.
   A.3. Gives examples or details to support main argument.
   A.4. Organizes ideas to support argument.
   A.5. Uses tone and voice to persuade.
   A.6. Observes grammar and usage conventions.

Chapter 4

Content Standards and Instructional Objectives

INSTRUCTIONAL OBJECTIVE:

Derives instructional objectives from state standards.

1. Describes characteristics of content standards.
2. Describes how content standards are expected to contribute to educational reform.
3. Describes the role of instructional objectives in a standards-based educational program.
4. Explains why instructional objectives should be developed cooperatively in a standard-based educational program.
5. States instructional objectives that clarify the intended learning outcomes of a content standard.

Since the *No Child Left Behind (NCLB)* Act of 2001, all states have established standards for student achievement. Many states had, or were working on, student achievement standards even before that. The NCLB Act requires that states report how well students have attained these standards. At this writing, the NCLB Act is up for reauthorization (in 2007); however, state content and performance standards are likely to be with us for a while. This chapter shows how to derive instructional objectives from standards.

Nature of Content Standards

States' content standards describe the content (facts, concepts, etc.) that students are expected to learn. Each standard may be followed by a listing of benchmarks that describe the knowledge and skills that represent achievement of the content standard. The content standards may be accompanied by performance level descriptors (PLDs) that describe what represents achievement. The content standards may be stated for selected levels in an educational program or be stated for each grade level.

Content standards specify what students are expected to learn, and focus on complex learning outcomes. The educational bar has been raised; these are complex learning outcomes, not "minimum competencies." Schools are expected to use the content standards to fashion the school curriculum, plan instruction, and prepare assessment instruments. Although the standards indicate the intended outcomes of instruction, teachers select the learning experiences and instructional strategies that they think are most appropriate. The use of state content standards as a framework for public education is a bold attempt to improve student achievement and move education to a level of excellence comparable to that of other countries that now lead in education.

Content standards vary widely in organization and in specificity. Some are broad, closer to what most textbooks would call "educational goals" than to the kind of instructional objectives this book describes. Others are very specific, perhaps only a step or two away from instructional objectives.

For the sake of illustration, we asked what fourth-grade mathematics teachers might find as expectations for what their students should learn about place value. We looked up the fourth-grade mathematics content standards for six states. We picked California, Hawaii, Montana, Nebraska, New York, and Pennsylvania. These states differ in size, geographical location, student demographics, and urban/rural composition. As it turns out, their content standards differ, too.

California (http://www.cde.ca.gov/be/st/ss/) has content standards for Mathematics for each grade K through 7, and for subjects (e.g., Albegra I) for grades 8–12. Grade 4 standards begin with a summary statement: "By the end of grade four, students understand large numbers and addition, subtraction, multiplication, and division of whole numbers. They describe and compare simple fractions and decimals. They understand the properties of, and the relationships between, plane geometric figures. They collect, represent, and analyze data to answer questions." Content standards are listed under five strands:

Number Sense (4 standards, with subdivisions);

Algebra and Functions (2 standards);

Measurement and Geometry (3 standards);

Statistics, Data Analysis, and Probability (2 standards); and

Mathematical Reasoning (3 standards).

Place value fits under one of the Number Sense standards, and we'll describe that more in the next section.

Hawaii (http://doe.k12.hi.us/standards/) has content and performance standards listed together in a searchable database. It has standards for Mathematics for each grade K through 8, and for subjects (e.g., Albegra I) for grades 9–12. Grade 4 lists 14 standards under five strands:

Numbers and Operations;

Measurement;

Geometry and Spatial Sense;

Patterns, Functions, and Algebra; and

Data Analysis, Statistics, and Probability.

Measurement and Geometry, which were considered in the same strand in California, are in separate strands in Hawaii. Mathematical Reasoning is not listed as a strand; however, Hawaii has six General Learner Outcomes for all students, one of which is Reasoning. Place value fits under one of the Numbers and Operations standards.

Montana (http://www.opi.state.mt.us/Accred/cstandards.html) has seven Mathematics Content Standards, with Benchmarks under each strand at grades 4, 8, and 12. The content standards are stated as sentences (e.g., "Students demonstrate understanding . . .") in the following areas, similar to what other states call strands:

Problem-solving and Reasoning;

Numbers and Operations;

Algebraic Concepts;

Geometry;

Measurement;

Data Analysis, Probability, and Statistics; and

Patterns, Relations, and Functions.

Montana also has Performance Standards at those three grade levels that describe performance required for designation as Advanced, Proficient, Nearing Proficiency, or Novice in Mathematics overall. Place value falls under Content Standard 2: "Students demonstrate understanding of and an ability to use numbers and operations."

Nebraska (http://www.nde.state.ne.us/ndestandards/AcademicStandards.htm) has Mathematics Content Standards and example indicators for grades K–1, 2–4, 5–8, and 9–12. These standards are grouped under 6 strands:

Numeration/Number Sense;

Computation/Estimation;

Measurement;

Geometry/Spatial Concepts;

Data Analysis, Probability, and Statistical Concepts; and

Algebraic Concepts.

Place value fits under Numeration/Number Sense.

New York (http://usny.nysed.gov/teachers/nyslearningstandards.html) organizes seven standards as Mathematics, Science, and Technology Standards. Several of these cross all three disciplines (e.g., "Standard 1: Students will use mathematical analysis, scientific inquiry, and engineering design, as appropriate, to pose questions, seek answers, and develop solutions."). Standard 3 is about mathematics content solely. Standard 3 has five Content Strands:

Number Sense and Operations,

Algebra,

Geometry,

Measurement, and

Statistics and Probability

and five Process Strands:

Problem Solving,

Reasoning and Proof,

Communication,

Connections, and

Representation.

The subdivisions under the content standards become quite a bit more specific than in the previous states, and the standards document is therefore longer. Place value fits under Number Sense and Operations. In the next section, we will illustrate how the specificity of these standards brings them closer to—although not always equivalent to—the general instructional objectives we describe in this text.

Pennsylvania (http://www.pde.state.pa.us/stateboard_ed/cwp/view.asp?a=3&Q=76716) describes 11 Mathematics Standards for four grade levels (grades 3, 5, 8, and 11). The 11 standards—although not called strands—are similar in content to the strands from other states:

Numbers, Number Systems and Number Relationships;

Computation and Estimation;

Measurement and Estimation;

Mathematical Reasoning and Connections;

Mathematical Problem Solving and Communication;

Statistics and Data Analysis;

Probability and Predictions;

Algebra and Functions;

Geometry;

Trigonometry;

Concepts of Calculus.

All standards, even Concepts of Calculus, have some statements for grades 3, 5, 8, and 11. This organizational structure contrasts with those of California and Hawaii, which change from strand-based standards at the elementary and intermediate levels to topic-based standards for high school. Place value fits under Numbers, Number Systems, and Number Relationships. Because our question is about fourth grade, we want to look at the standards for both grades 3 and 5.

You can look up any state's content standards on the Web. Locate the state's Department of Education or Office of Public Instruction (or whatever your state calls its education department) Web page, and follow links for assessment, accountability, or standards. You should know at least your own state's standards for the content area and grade level you teach or in which you do fieldwork, if you are a teacher education student. Comparisons can be helpful, too, especially at the level of subdivisions under the standards. These can help you understand what knowledge and skills are commonly considered important in each content area.

Be prepared to find a lot of variation. Mathematics standards are arguably more consistent from state to state than other content standards. In fact, that's why we used Math for our example, so that there wouldn't be an overwhelming amount of variation to describe. And yet look how much variation we found in Mathematics content standards. Just wait until the next section! The differences increase as you drill down into the specific statements under the standards, as you will see for our place value example—again chosen to be about as simple an example as possible.

Need for Instructional Objectives

The benchmarks or subdivisions listed under content standards are frequently stated in terms of *knows, understands, applies, evaluates,* or some relevant skill. The statements include the content to be learned or the nature of the skill but not specifically how learning will be shown. How do students demonstrate that they know, understand, can apply, evaluate, or perform the skill? Sometimes a standard's benchmarks or performance level objectives clarify the general outcome stated in the standard, but more specific learning outcomes need to be stated to clarify what the students can do when they have mastered the content.

Our question about place value may have implied that you should look to standards to find out where to "put" things in your curriculum. We didn't mean to imply that; we just needed a way to offer a concrete illustration of the wide variation in standards. In fact, standards are intended to be used in the opposite direction. District curriculum developers and teachers should look at the standards and reason from them to the curricular content, goals, and objectives that should be organized to meet them.

With that caution, let's return to our illustration. If we were fourth-grade mathematics teachers who teach place value, how would we specify our instructional objectives to fit in the state's standards-based system? What are students expected to know and be able to do with place value?

Figure 4.1 shows the place-value bits from each of our six sample states. We have taken just small bits for the sake of a manageable illustration. Other standards could also be relevant, for example, problem solving and reasoning standards using place-value content. And other parts of the state standards documents (benchmarks, sample performance indicators, performance level descriptors, rubrics) could also be relevant. Notice that even

Figure 4.1   Excerpts from Content Standards Describing Intentions for Learning about Place Value by the Fourth Grade, from Six States

---

CALIFORNIA

Number Sense
1.0 Students understand the place value of whole numbers and decimals to two decimal places and how whole numbers and decimals relate to simple fractions. Students use the concepts of negative numbers:
   1.1 Read and write whole numbers in the millions.
   1.2 Order and compare whole numbers and decimals to two decimal places.
   1.3 Round whole numbers through the millions to the nearest ten, hundred, thousand, ten thousand, or hundred thousand.
   1.6 Write tenths and hundredths in decimal and fraction notations and know the fraction and decimal equivalents for halves and fourths (e.g., 1/2 = 0.5 or .50; 7/4 = 1 3/4 = 1.75).

HAWAII

Standard 1: Numbers and Operations: NUMBER SENSE—Understand numbers, ways of representing numbers, relationships among numbers, and number systems
Benchmark MA.4.1.1 Identify place value from ten-thousandths to millions
Sample performance assessment: The student identifies the value of a digit in a number (e.g., identifies the value of each of the 7's in the number 7,370,892.871).

MONTANA

Content Standard 2 — Students demonstrate understanding of and an ability to use numbers and operations.
   Benchmark 2 for content standard 2, by End of Grade 4 —
   Use the number system by counting, grouping and applying place value concepts.

NEBRASKA

4.1 Numeration/Number Sense
   4.1.1 By the end of fourth grade, students will demonstrate place value of whole numbers through the millions and decimals to the hundredth place.
   Example indicators:
       • Read and write numerals (in digits and words) through the one millions place and decimals to the hundredth place.
       • Order and compare whole numbers through the one millions place and decimals to the hundredths place using the symbols <, >, and =.
       • Round whole numbers to the nearest named place, such as rounding 1,234 to the nearest hundred would be 1,200.

Continued

Figure 4.1   Excerpts from Content Standards Describing Intentions for Learning about Place Value by the Fourth Grade, from Six States (*Continued*)

NEW YORK

Number Sense & Operations Strand
Students will understand numbers, multiple ways of representing numbers, relationships among numbers, and number systems.

Number Systems	4.N.4	Understand the place value structure of the base ten number system:
		10 ones = 1 ten
		10 tens = 1 hundred
		10 hundreds = 1 thousand
		10 thousands = 1 ten thousand
	4.N.10	Develop an understanding of decimals as part of a whole
	4.N.11	Read and write decimals to hundredths, using money as a context
	4.N.12	Use concrete materials and visual models to compare and order decimals (less than 1) to the hundredths place in the context of money

---

PENNSYLVANIA

2.1.   Numbers, Number Systems and Number Relationships

2.1.3. **GRADE 3**

    I. Apply place-value concepts and numeration to counting, ordering and grouping.

2.1.5. **GRADE 5**

    A. Use expanded notation to represent whole numbers or decimals.

---

with the simplest approach and very basic content (place value), there is enormous variation in the amount and kind of information you get from the state standard from which you derive your district's curricular goals and your instructional objectives.

We are not endorsing one kind of standards over another. There are advantages and disadvantages to both broad standards and narrow ones. Different states used different processes to arrive at their standards. Different states assess their standards differently. The purpose of the comparison in Figure 4.1 is to illustrate the range you will find in standards, so that you will be prepared to teach in any state and to deal with all kinds of different standards.

All six states in Figure 4.1 would like students to know about place value by fourth grade (in Pennsylvania, by third grade). Four specify how many places (California, hundredths to millions; Hawaii, ten-thousandths to millions; Nebraska, hundredths to millions; New York, hundredths to ten-thousands). Two (Montana and Pennsylvania) don't.

The verbs used to indicate the nature of the target achievement differ, too. California's standard says "understand place value." Hawaii's and New York's standards say "understand numbers," and put place-value benchmarks with various verbs under that. Nebraska's standard reads "demonstrate place value." Pennsylvania and Montana say "apply place value concepts." In the strict sense of the verbs' meanings, these are different expectations. Indeed, throughout this book we encourage you to really pay attention to your own verbs in order to be very clear about what you want students to know and be able to do. However, not all state standards will be so exacting in their use of verbs. We doubt, for example, that Pennsylvania and Montana are the only states that want students to be able to apply place-value concepts. When California specifies understanding, they no doubt want students to be able to use that understanding, too. And so on.

So that's the first lesson. Don't look to state content standards for instructional objectives–style use of verbs. Look to state content standards for—you guessed it—content. Of course, pay attention to the verbs, but don't take them as literally as we are encouraging you to use them when you write your own instructional objectives.

The second lesson is about the amount of specificity. Notice the range. Montana's "Use the number system by counting, grouping and applying place value concepts" would need to be broken down over several levels to reach the appropriate level of generality for instructional objectives to be used in classroom lessons. At the other extreme, New York's "Read and write decimals to hundredths, using money as a context" are about at the level of two (reading and writing, respectively) specific learning outcomes under a general instructional objective about knowing or understanding decimals to the hundredths place.

The same procedures for specifying the specific learning outcomes described in Chapters 1 and 2 apply here. Where the benchmarks are general (e.g., knows), define them in more definite terms that specify the precise nature of the student performance (see Figure 4.2 for some types of verbs to use). These specific learning outcomes provide more definite direction for both teaching and assessment. The content standards make clear what the students should know and the instructional objectives clarify what is meant by knowing.

When the benchmarks are stated in such specific terms as *identifies, describes, explains,* or *predicts*, the statements may be used directly as intended learning outcomes. In any event, in a standard-based educational program, it is important to state instructional objectives that are in harmony with the content standards and that clearly describe the types of student performance that represent mastery of the standards.

Instructional objectives like the following might be useful in lessons in any of these states. Depending on the state, the range of place values required might change. For example, in New York the objective might read "ten-thousands" instead of "millions." In each state, however, it would require a different number of intermediate goals to get from this instructional objective to the state standard.

1. Knows place value locations in the base-10 number system.

   1.1. Identifies decimals to hundredths.

   1.2. Identifies place value of whole numbers to ten-thousands.

Figure 4.2   Some Sample Verbs to Use in Converting Benchmarks to Instructional Objectives

Knows	Defines, describes, explains, identifies, labels, lists, matches, names, outlines, reproduces, selects, states
Understands	Converts, defends, distinguishes, estimates, extends, general-izes, gives examples, infers, paraphrases, produces, rewrites, summarizes
Applies	Changes, computes, demonstrates, discovers, manipulates, modi-fies, operates, predicts, prepares, produces, relates, shows, solves, uses
Evaluates	Appraises, compares, concludes, contrasts, criticizes, describes, discriminates, explains, justifies, interprets, relates, summarizes, supports
Performance Skills	Arranges, assembles, builds, calibrates, changes, constructs, demonstrates, displays, fastens, fixes, manipulates, measures, mixes, organizes, revises, solves, uses
Thinking Skills	Analyzes, arranges, associates, classifies, distinguishes between, estimates, formulates, generates, identifies, infers, judges, relates, synthesizes, verifies

    1.3. Reads decimals to hundredths.

    1.4. Writes decimals to hundredths.

    1.5. Reads whole numbers to millions.

    1.6. Writes whole numbers to millions.

2. Understands place value concepts.

    2.1. Orders whole numbers to millions and decimals to hundredths using $<$, $>$, and $=$.

    2.2. Identifies decimals equivalent to the fractions ½ and ¼.

    2.3. Rounds whole numbers to the nearest ten, hundred, thousand, ten thousand, or hundred thousand.

    2.4. Uses visuals to order and compare sums of money with decimals to the hundredths place.

    2.5. Explains how decimals represent parts of a whole.

    2.6. Uses diagrams to demonstrate the base-10 relationships among ones, tens, hundreds, . . . , millions.

The more general the state standard, and the more levels of abstraction between the state standard and classroom instructional objectives, the more room there is for teacher interpretation. In a state-based program, it is desirable to develop instructional objectives cooperatively. This increases the likelihood that all teachers at the same grade level, or teaching the same subject, will be focusing on the same intended learning outcomes. It also helps clarify the desired changes in student performance from one instructional level to the next. Of course, it also makes possible the sharing of instructional strategies and assessment procedures that are most effective. State content standards provide a broad framework for developing the curriculum and planning the instructional program but cooperative effort is needed to make it effective in improving the learning of students.

Summary

1. Content standards are general goals that indicate what students are expected to learn. Many professional organizations and most states have prepared content standards for the various subjects taught in the schools.

2. States' content standards vary considerably. Some are very broad umbrellas under which many instructional objectives fall. Others are more specific.

3. Content standards and benchmarks are typically stated in general terms (e.g., knows, understands) and need to be clarified by more specific instructional objectives. Thus, the content standards provide a framework for developing the curriculum and planning the instructional program, but specifically stated instructional objectives are needed for teaching and assessment.

4. Content standards typically focus on complex learning outcomes that all students are expected to master. They attempt to improve the quality of education by demanding a higher level of achievement at all levels of education. Instructional objectives must reflect this emphasis on higher-level learning outcomes.

5. Cooperative development of instructional objectives, classroom activities, and assessment procedures will provide greater assurance that teachers at the same grade level, or teaching the same subject, will be focusing on the same intended learning outcomes and using relevant strategies and assessment procedures to achieve them.

Exercises

1. Select two states (other than our six examples) and find what their content standards have to say about learning place value. Using your examples as well as ours, discuss the characteristics of content standards.

2. Figure 4.1 shows that Montana's content Benchmark 2 for Standard 2 reads that by the end of grade 4, students will "Use the number system by counting, grouping, and applying place value concepts." State several general instructional objectives and associated specific learning outcomes that clarify these intended outcomes at an appropriate level of specificity to use for classroom instruction and assessment.

Chapter 5

Considerations in Preparing Instructional Objectives

INSTRUCTIONAL OBJECTIVE:

Uses appropriate resources and criteria to prepare high-quality instructional objectives.

1. States the advantages of using a frame of reference when preparing objectives.
2. Describes the sources for locating lists of objectives developed by others.
3. Lists the factors to consider when evaluating the final list of objectives.
4. Describes the advantages of developing objectives cooperatively.
5. Writes sample instructional objectives for a given category of intended learning outcomes.

Now that you have been exposed to the method of stating objectives as intended learning outcomes and their use in planning for instruction and assessment, let's take a look at the process of preparing a list of objectives for a given unit or course of instruction. How do you get started? What are some of the considerations? Where can you get ideas for objectives? How do you select and review objectives for the final list? In other words, how do you put it all together so that you can prepare an appropriate list of objectives for some instructional area?

Using a Frame of Reference as a Guide

When you prepare instructional objectives, it is helpful to refer to some frame of reference that clarifies the various types of learning outcomes to consider. In the last chapter, we noted that in a standard-based educational program the content standards for each grade level provide the framework for writing instructional objectives. Even in educational programs in other areas (e.g., private schools, colleges, and military schools), you still need a frame of reference to guide the selection and writing of instructional objectives. This will provide greater assurance that all important objectives, ranging from simple to complex, are considered.

A simple framework like that in Figure 5.1 illustrates the wide array of learning outcomes that might be included in any given instructional area. It makes clear that there are many desirable learning outcomes that go beyond the simple knowledge and skill outcomes. The recent focus on complex cognitive outcomes, problem solving, and performance skills makes it imperative that objectives be considered in all of these areas.

Much more detailed and highly structured is the *Taxonomy of Educational Objectives* developed by teachers, psychologists, and test experts. It provides an older, but still useful, comprehensive framework for identifying and writing instructional objectives. The *Taxonomy* was recently revised (Anderson & Krathwohl, 2001) into a two-dimensional framework that considers types of knowledge and cognitive processes separately.

Webb's (2002, 2007) Depth of Knowledge framework was developed for use in studies of the alignment between state assessments and the state standards they were designed to measure. Because of its widespread use in alignment studies, this framework comes

Figure 5.1   Types of Learning Outcomes Common to Many Areas and Levels of Instruction

Lower-Level Cognitive Outcomes Knowledge Comprehension Application	Recalling Translating Interpreting Estimating Comparing Classifying Applying
Higher-Level Thinking Skills Analysis Synthesis Evaluation	Identifying Analyzing Inferring Relating Formulating Generating Judging
Affective Outcomes Attitudes Interests Appreciations Adjustments	Listening Responding Participating Seeking Demonstrating Relating Valuing
Performance Outcomes Procedure Product Procedure and product Problem solving	Speaking Singing Drawing Computing Writing Constructing Demonstrating Operating Performing Originating

to describe the expected nature of the things students can do to demonstrate their achievement of standards. Therefore, this framework is useful to consider for the curricular goals and instructional objectives based on those standards.

In the following sections, we describe the original and revised *Taxonomy of Educational Objectives* and the Webb Depth of Knowledge levels. There are several other frameworks you could use. See Nitko and Brookhart (2007) or Gronlund (2006) for descriptions of several of these.

Taxonomy of Educational Objectives

The developers of *Taxonomy of Educational Objectives* attempted to identify all possible educational outcomes and classify them by general and specific categories, in a hierarchical pattern, somewhat like the classification of plants and animals.

The developers of the *Taxonomy* identified three domains of the educational outcomes: cognitive, affective, and psychomotor.

1. *Cognitive:* Concerned with intellectual outcomes; the classification system ranges from lower-level knowledge outcomes to higher-level intellectual abilities and skills (Bloom, Englehard, Furst, Hill, & Krathwohl, 1956).

2. *Affective:* Concerned with outcomes in the areas of interests, attitudes, appreciation, and methods of adjustment, using a classification system ranging from receiving stimuli to developing a characteristic set of values that directs behavior (Krathwohl, Bloom, & Masia, 1964).

3. *Psychomotor:* Concerned with motor skills; one classification system (Simpson, 1972) ranges from perception of cues to origination of a new movement pattern.

The originators of the *Taxonomy* developed a complete classification system for the cognitive and affective domains but did not complete the psychomotor domain system as scheduled. Other individuals, however, not connected with the original taxonomy developers, have prepared classification systems for the psychomotor domain (Harrow, 1972; Simpson, 1972). We selected Simpson's for our use so that all three domains of the taxonomy could be presented.

The categories and subcategories in each of the three domains are arranged in hierarchical order, from the simplest outcomes to the most complex. This arrangement required the use of new terminology that can be confusing at first; however, a classification system with a distinctive set of hierarchical categories requires clearly defined, limited terminology. The cognitive domain, for example, includes the categories of knowledge, comprehension, application, analysis, synthesis, and evaluation. Note that the categories of the cognitive domain do not use such traditional terminology as *understanding* and *thinking* because these terms cut across categories. For example, understanding can be shown by performance at the comprehension or the application level. High-level thinking skills are covered by the top several levels of the cognitive domain.

The affective domain includes the categories of receiving, responding, valuing, organization, and characterization by a value or value complex. The traditional categories of interest, attitude, appreciation, and modes of adjustment overlap several of these taxonomy categories. Similarly, the psychomotor domain uses a set of categories ranging from simple to complex and the typical motor skills overlap several categories depending on the student's stage of development.

The three domains of the taxonomy provide a comprehensive and clearly structured classification system that provides a good frame of reference for preparing instructional objectives. But don't feel you must use the terminology of the taxonomy categories when writing objectives. You can state objectives in many ways, and how you state them is determined somewhat by the nature of the subject or skill area.

The taxonomy can be most useful in helping you (1) get ideas for types of objectives to consider, ranging from simple to complex, (2) arrange the objectives in terms of complexity, and (3) check on the completeness of the final set of objectives. It is important to keep in mind, however, that the taxonomy is arranged in terms of complexity and not difficulty. This will prevent you from thinking that complex outcomes such as thinking and reasoning cannot be taught until later in an educational program. These so-called "higher level" learning outcomes can be taught at any age level and to students with various educational backgrounds. Another caution is that instructional objectives frequently include specific learning outcomes from more than one domain. For example, a skill outcome may include all three categories: knowing what to do, skill in doing it, and proceeding in a safe manner. So, use a taxonomy as a guide and not a restrictive framework.

Useful summaries of the main categories in the three domains of the taxonomy are presented in Appendix B. Each category is briefly described and illustrated with lists of sample objectives and verbs for stating the specific learning outcomes. The original references from which the summaries were derived are also included for those who wish to study the taxonomy in more detail.

Many teachers use the original *Taxonomy of Educational Objectives* because that's the framework they learned to use, and because it's very useful. The older taxonomy has now been revised (Anderson & Krathwohl, 2001) and uses a two-dimensional framework. The two dimensions treat type of knowledge (the Knowledge Dimension) and type of thinking (the Cognitive Process Dimension) separately. The content to be learned is classified into one of four categories of Knowledge: Factual Knowledge, Conceptual Knowledge, Procedural Knowledge, and Metacognitive Knowledge. The kind of thinking required is classified into one of six categories of Cognitive Process: Remember, Understand, Apply, Analyze, Evaluate, and Create. A two-dimensional table places each specific learning outcome and assessment tasks or items on both dimensions (see Appendix C).

Webb's Depth of Knowledge Framework

Developed to support an alignment process that maps state assessments to the standards they are designed to measure, Depth of Knowledge levels indicate the complexity of thinking required for a learning goal or an assessment task. As such, they are similar in purpose to the Cognitive Process Dimension of the Anderson and Krathwohl (2001) taxonomy described above. They are commonly used in alignment studies of state assessments. Appendix D presents a chart with examples that have been used in state alignment studies (Webb, 2002).

Level 1, Recall, involves remembering facts or concepts or doing simple, one-step procedures. In math, applying one formula to solve a math problem would be an example of a one-step Level 1 task. In reading, looking up a word in the dictionary or identifying a simile in a passage would be an example of a one-step Level 1 task. Verbs at this level include *identify*, *recall*, *recognize*, *use*, and *measure*. Verbs like *describe* and *explain* could be used at different levels, depending on the nature of the description or explanation required.

Level 2, Skill/Concept, requires mental processing beyond simple recall. Level 2 responses require students to make a decision about how to approach the problem. The procedure is not rote as in Level 1. A Level 2 example in math might be comparing information from two different graphs. In reading, a Level 2 example might be identifying and summarizing the main ideas in a passage. Verbs at this level include *classify*, *organize*, *estimate*, *make observations*, *collect and display data*, and *compare*.

Level 3, Strategic Thinking, involves reasoning, planning, and using evidence. Tasks that ask students to explain their reasoning are often at Level 3. In math or science, using concepts to solve complex problems is an example of a Level 3 task. In reading or social studies, using information from multiple sources to address a question or topic is an example of a Level 3 task.

Level 4, Extended Thinking, requires planning and extended work over time. Time itself is not a factor if lower-level work is simply repeated (for example, looking up a new word each day to compile a personal dictionary). Examples of Level 4 tasks include designing and conducting experiments or analyzing and synthesizing information from a variety of sources.

Cautions in Using Any Framework as a Guide

The various frames of reference provide useful guides for identifying and writing instructional objectives. They help you obtain a more comprehensive and well-balanced list of intended learning outcomes. However, don't blindly follow any classification system. There is no need to develop objectives in an area just because it is listed in some framework. The nature of the course, the goals of the school program, and the curriculum guide should shape your final list of objectives. Use the various classification systems in a creative way—to get ideas, to expand your list of outcomes, and to organize your objectives in some meaningful manner.

Other Guides in Preparing Instructional Objectives

You can use a number of sources for identifying, writing, and organizing objectives in a given area of instruction. The following sources should help you get started in your teaching area.

Curriculum Guides

Some libraries keep files of curriculum guides for teachers in training. You might find it useful to review a number of different guides, if they are available, to note the variation in coverage and the way the objectives are stated. If you are already teaching, or know where you will be teaching, you of course will want to consult any curriculum guide available in your district.

Books and Special Reports

Many books on methods of teaching discuss objectives, present illustrative lists, and contain references that will help you locate others. The yearbooks and other references published by the National Council of Teachers of English, the National Council of Teachers of Mathematics, the National Council for the Social Studies, and the National Science Teachers Association also contain suggested lists of objectives from time to time. The more recent publications will give greater emphasis to the thinking-problem-solving type of curriculum, and the method of stating the intended learning outcomes will reflect this emphasis. These and other organizations have also published sets of standards that are available (see Figure 5.2).

Textbooks and instructional materials at the elementary level typically contain lists of objectives for each lesson. However, they tend to focus on limited and detailed elements of content and are not always stated in performance terms (e.g., "Understand that living things need water"). These lesson-plan type of objectives can serve as a source of ideas for preparing instructional objectives for an area of instruction, if broadened (e.g., "Comprehends the elements needed to sustain life") and defined in performance terms (e.g., "Identifies the elements needed," "Explains the role of each element," "Describes what happens when there is a shortage of a particular element"). Objectives and specific learning outcomes such as these are more useful for planning both the instruction and the assessment of intended learning outcomes, and can also serve as a guide for more detailed statements for lesson plans.

An especially helpful guide is McREL's Compendium of K–12 content standards and benchmarks, the result of comparing and contrasting the content standards from all the states. This compendium (http://www.mcrel.org/standards-benchmarks/) is presented in both searchable and browsable formats. The Web site includes tools and resources for developing standards-based units and lessons.

Figure 5.2   Sources of Standards for Various Subject Domains

---

National Council of Teachers of English and the International Reading Association. *Standards for the English Language Arts.* Urbana, Illinois: National Council of Teachers of English, 1996.
www.ncte.org

National Council of Teachers of Mathematics. *Principles and Standards for School Mathematics.* Reston, Virginia: National Council of Teachers of Mathematics, Inc., 2000.
www.nctm.org

National Council for the Social Studies. *Expectations of Excellence: Curriculum Standards for Social Studies.* Washington, D.C.: National Council for the Social Studies, 1994.
www.ncss.org

National Research Council. *National Science Education Standards.* Washington, D.C.: National Academy Press, 1996.
www.nationalacademies.org

National Standards in Foreign Language Project. *Standards for Foreign Language Learning: Preparing for the 21st Century* (3rd ed.). Lawrence, Kansas: Allen Press, 2006.
www.actfl.org

Test Manuals

Some recent achievement test batteries focus on curriculum standards in the various sub-jects suggested by the National Councils, discussed earlier, and by various commissions and curriculum projects. The test manuals, or separate publications, typically include statements of the learning outcomes being assessed, and thus provide another source of ideas for identifying and stating instructional objectives in your area of teaching. Empha-sis in some of these recent achievement test manuals is on thinking, problem solving, and the use of realistic situations. Just remember that the intended learning outcomes stressed in achievement test batteries are those common to many schools nationwide, and there-fore may not include those unique to a local instructional program.

Considerations in Selecting Instructional Objectives

It is usually possible to identify many more instructional objectives than can be achieved in a particular course or instructional unit. The constraints of time, teaching resources, and prerequisites to the instruction limit what you can expect students to learn. Thus these and other factors must be considered in compiling the final list. The following questions will serve as criteria for reviewing and selecting the most appro-priate objectives to include. They can also be a guide for an ongoing review of objec-tives during instruction to make sure that they remain in harmony with teaching and assessment.

Do the Objectives Indicate Learning Outcomes That Are Appropriate to the Instructional Area?

This question has no simple answers, but it has to be considered. Your state standards and district curriculum are the first places to look. If your state's standards are clear statements of instructional goals, you may find it's a fairly straightforward walk from standards to instructional objectives (see Chapter 4). Where the standards are vague or lend them-selves to a wide variety of interpretations, you can turn to the recommendations of experts in the curriculum area in which you plan to teach. What learning outcomes do they con-sider to be most important? There will not be complete agreement here, but a review of their recommendations will help you identify the objectives that have the support of most curriculum specialists. This review will prevent any serious omissions and will provide greater assurance that your final list of objectives is in harmony with the most recent de-velopments in the area.

Do the Objectives Represent All Logical Learning Outcomes of the Instructional Area?

Here we are concerned with the comprehensiveness and representativeness of the list of objectives. For example, are objectives included from all three areas of learning—

cognitive, affective, and psychomotor? Does a proper balance exist among the three areas and within each area? Teachers in areas where intellectual skills are dominant have a tendency to overemphasize knowledge of specific facts and to neglect complex intellectual outcomes, attitudes, interests, and skills. On the other hand, teachers in areas where performance skills are dominant (art, music, physical education) often neglect the cognitive outcomes to be achieved.

Are the Objectives Attainable by These Particular Students?

The nature of the student group and their readiness for particular learning experiences are important considerations in formulating and selecting objectives. Pre-assessments, including simple discussions, can help you discover what background and learning experiences students have with the instructional objectives you plan to teach.

Closely related concerns are the time allowed for the instruction and the facilities and teaching materials available. The development of thinking skills and changes in attitude, for example, are extremely time consuming because they depend on the cumulative effect of a long series of learning experiences. Similarly, some outcomes (e.g., skill in the scientific method) may require special laboratory facilities and teaching materials. We are not suggesting that otherwise desirable objectives be discarded, but simply that they may need to be modified to fit the student group and the instructional conditions under which they are to be achieved.

Are the Objectives in Harmony with the Philosophy of the School in Which the Instruction Is to Be Given?

This would be an easy criterion to apply if each school had a clear statement of philosophy or a list of educational goals to serve as a guide. Unfortunately, some schools do not; you must infer which outcomes are most valued in such schools. If a school appears to emphasize independent work, self-discipline, freedom to explore new areas, and the democratic planning of activities, for example, these emphases should be reflected in the final list of instructional objectives. Similarly, if every teacher is expected to stress effective oral and written communication, thinking skills, and complex performance tasks, a broader range of instructional objectives will need to be included than might otherwise be the case. In short, your instructional objectives should be in harmony with the stated or implicit goals of the total school program.

Are the Objectives in Harmony with Basic Principles of Learning?

As we indicated earlier, instructional objectives should be stated as desired learning outcomes. Therefore, it is legitimate to ask to what extent your objectives are in harmony with what is known about the principles of learning. Some of the basic factors that should be considered are the following:

1. *Readiness:* Are the students mature enough to attain these particular objectives? Do the students have the necessary experiences and educational background to proceed successfully? Is there another level at which some of the objectives might be attained more readily?

2. *Motivation:* Do these objectives reflect the needs and interests of the students? Can they be restated or modified to be more closely related to the students' concerns? Is there another stage of development where these objectives would more closely fit the students' emerging interests?

3. *Retention:* Do these objectives reflect learning outcomes that tend to be retained longest (e.g., comprehension, application, thinking skills)? Are there other objectives that might be more lasting and that should be included?

4. *Transfer Value:* Do these objectives reflect learning outcomes that are widely applicable to new situations? Do the objectives include methods of study and modes of thinking that are most likely to contribute to future learning in the area? Do the objectives reflect realistic and complex learning tasks that are most useful in the "real" world?

These questions are not always easily answered, but they highlight the importance of considering the learning process when you formulate and select instructional objectives. Most general textbooks on educational psychology will provide extended discussions of the basic learning principles. It is sufficient to point out here that the more complex learning outcomes tend to be retained longer and to have greater transfer value. When they are appropriate to the developmental level of the learner, the more complex outcomes also have the greatest potential for arousing and maintaining student interest.

Preparing Instructional Objectives Cooperatively

As pointed out in Chapter 4, "Content Standards and Instructional Objectives," it is desirable to have teachers prepare lists of instructional objectives cooperatively wherever possible. This might involve teachers at the same grade level or in the same department working together, or it might involve committees of teachers representing all grade levels and all departments in the school. Cooperative development of objectives will ease the burden because the work can be divided among the teachers. In addition, this procedure provides greater assurance that (1) teachers of the same curriculum are emphasizing the same learning outcomes, (2) the sequence of instructional objectives from one grade level to the next or one course to the next is appropriate, (3) a minimum of overlap exists in single-course objectives (e.g., knowledge of facts), and (4) proper attention is given to multiple-course objectives (e.g., reasoning ability) in each teacher's lists.

Summary

1. A frame of reference that classifies the various types of learning outcomes can aid in identifying, stating, and organizing objectives into an appropriate list. It is especially useful in clarifying the broad range of complex learning outcomes that should be considered.

2. The *Taxonomy of Educational Objectives* is an older framework but it provides the most comprehensive and complete classification of cognitive, affective, and psychomotor objectives. A 2001 revision of the cognitive portion of the *Taxonomy* uses a two-dimensional classification scheme.

3. Webb's Depth of Knowledge levels are often used to classify the level of thinking needed for state standards and the assessments that measure them. This is a useful framework to use for instructional objectives that are derived from state standards if the state assessment has been aligned to the standards using this framework.

4. Aid in preparing a list of objectives for an instructional area can also be obtained by consulting lists of objectives and standards prepared by others. These can be found in curriculum guides, methods books, the publications of the National Councils in each subject area, and achievement test manuals.

5. Check your final list of instructional objectives for appropriateness, representativeness, attainability, relevance to the institution's instructional program, and relevance to the basic principles of learning.

6. In school settings, prepare instructional objectives cooperatively with other teachers to ensure uniformity within grade levels and proper sequencing between grade levels.

Exercises

1. Mr. Jones didn't bother using a frame of reference to prepare his instructional objectives. "Hmf!" he said to Ms. Smith one day. "Much ado about nothing. I'll just teach." Ms. Smith wanted to convince Mr. Jones that it was worthwhile to use a frame of reference. What are some points she should make for this argument?

2. Write sample instructional objectives for at least one of the following categories of intended learning outcomes.

   a. Apply place-value concepts and numeration to counting, ordering, and grouping (Pennsylvania Mathematics Standard 2.1.3).

   b. Apply conventions of standard written English (e.g. spelling, punctuation, usage) appropriate for grade level and purpose (Montana Writing Content Standard 1, Benchmark 4).

Part II

Writing Instructional Objectives for Various Outcomes

Chapter 6

Writing Objectives for Knowledge, Comprehension, and Application Outcomes

INSTRUCTIONAL OBJECTIVE:

Writes objectives for knowledge, comprehension, and application outcomes.

1. Describes the characteristics of learning outcomes at the knowledge, comprehension, and application levels.
2. Writes illustrative general instructional objectives for each of the three categories of objectives.
3. Writes sample general objectives and specific learning outcomes to illustrate how objectives can be adapted to different *areas* of instruction.
4. Writes sample general objectives and specific learning outcomes to illustrate how objectives can be adapted to different *levels* of instruction.
5. Writes different versions of the same instructional objectives for some intended learning outcome.

Although the major emphasis is on thinking, problem solving, and other complex learning outcomes in education, learning programs are still concerned with objectives at the knowledge, comprehension, and application levels. After all, students have to think *about* something.

Knowledge outcomes are concerned with the recall or recognition of learned material. Comprehension is concerned with grasping the meaning of material as shown by interpretation, translation, prediction, and similar responses. Application is the ability to use the material in new situations. All three levels may be concerned with terms, facts, rules, procedures, concepts, principles, or theories.

Most content areas and levels of instruction include some emphasis on intended learning outcomes at the knowledge, comprehension, and application levels. In some cases

Figure 6.1   Sample General Instructional Objectives

Examples of knowledge, comprehension, and application outcomes in various content areas.

Mathematics
   Knows the meaning of terms and symbols.
   Comprehends mathematics concepts and processes.
   Applies concepts and processes to mathematical problems.

Reading
   Knows word meanings.
   Comprehends the literal meaning of written material.
   Applies reading skills to textbook material.

Writing
   Knows the mechanics of writing.
   Comprehends grammatical rules of writing.
   Applies writing skills in laboratory reports.

Science
   Knows scientific terms.
   Comprehends scientific concepts and principles.
   Applies concepts and principles.

Social Studies
   Knows facts about social problems.
   Comprehends effects of social problems on society.
   Applies problem-solving approach to social problems.

these terms can be used directly in the statements of general instructional objectives, as shown in Figure 6.1.

In others, the statements may fit the instruction more closely if different terminology is used and the categories are simply used as a general framework. The following example illustrates this at the elementary level of instruction.

1. Knows geometric shapes (knowledge).
   1.1. Draws a given shape (e.g., circle, square).
   1.2. Selects an object representing a given shape (e.g., ball, box).
   1.3. Identifies shapes of objects in a picture (e.g., building, lake).
   1.4. Describes objects using the names of shapes.

2. Interprets graphs (comprehension).
   2.1. Identifies the value of a given position on a graph.
   2.2. Identifies the relative values of two given positions on a graph.
   2.3. Describes the trend indicated by a graph.
   2.4. Distinguishes between statements that are supported and unsupported by a graph.

3. Solves word problems (application).
   3.1. Selects the proper procedure.

    3.2. Estimates the approximate result.

    3.3. Calculates the answer and compares with approximation.

    3.4. Checks the answer using another method.

There are many ways to state a general instructional objective, and the specific learning outcomes clarify the types of student performance that represent achievement of the objective.

Stating Objectives at the Knowledge, Comprehension, and Application Levels

The level of learning expected deepens as you go from knowledge to comprehension to application. The following objectives for a common outcome, the learning of terms, illustrates how the specific learning outcomes clarify the types of performance that characterize each level.

1. Knows common terms.
   1.1. Identifies a definition of the term.
   1.2. Identifies an example of the term.
   1.3. Writes a synonym of the term.
   1.4. Writes an antonym of the term.

2. Comprehends the meaning of terms.
   2.1. Defines a term in own words.
   2.2. Distinguishes between correct and incorrect use of a term.
   2.3. Explains the meaning of a term in light of its contextual setting.
   2.4. Describes the similarities and differences between two terms similar in meaning.

3. Applies terms in written work.
   3.1. Selects the term that best describes an idea, action, or event.
   3.2. Writes a sentence using a given term.
   3.3. Writes a paragraph using a given set of terms.
   3.4. Uses new terms in assigned writing projects.

Describing the intended learning outcomes at each level makes it possible to identify students who know the material (e.g., by memorizing) but don't understand it well enough to put it in their own words, identify examples of it, or apply it in some way.

In some cases the general objectives can be defined by specific learning outcomes that are useful in different areas of instruction and at several levels of instruction, as shown in our illustrative list. More commonly, however, the list of specific learning outcomes needs to be modified to reflect the specific types of performance expected from the instruction.

Adapting Statements to Areas of Instruction

Although it is desirable in stating and defining instructional objectives to keep the statements general enough to be useful with various units of study, they should be closely adapted to the instructional area. For example, in writing specific learning outcomes for "Knows common terms" in mathematics, the following list of specific learning outcomes might be used.

1. Knows common terms (math).
    1.1. Identifies the symbol that represents the term.
    1.2. Describes the procedure indicated by the term.
    1.3. Names the parts of a given problem.
    1.4. Writes a formula that represents the term.

Similarly, comprehension objectives in different subjects might be adapted as follows:

1. Comprehends science principles.
    1.1. Identifies the principle in restated form.
    1.2. Describes examples of the principle.
    1.3. States hypotheses that are in harmony with the principle.
    1.4. Distinguishes between correct and incorrect interpretations of the principle.

2. Comprehends mathematics principles and procedures.
    2.1. Writes mathematical formulas from given verbal statements.
    2.2. Explains why a given procedure is selected to solve a particular problem.
    2.3. Describes a method for checking answers.
    2.4. States the principle on which a given operation is based.

Learning outcomes at the comprehension and application levels seem most appropriate for such content areas as science, mathematics, and social studies but less useful in courses emphasizing simple performance skills. A course like keyboarding, for example, stresses primarily knowledge and skill outcomes, and there is little value in attempting to force the outcomes into the more complex categories of comprehension and application. Keyboarding is an application of skill but this type of application is not the same as the "application" category we have been describing. The latter refers to the use of principles to solve problems that are new to the students. Thus it represents a higher level of understanding than comprehension, and does not refer to the application of performance skills as in keyboarding.

Knowledge and skill play a major role in several areas. For example, at the elementary level, such areas as speaking, spelling, and simple computation skills would fall in this category. At the secondary level such courses as art, music, vocational courses, and physical education might include complex learning outcomes in some areas, but also have some that place major emphasis on knowledge and skill. Stating outcomes in the area of performance skills will be described in a later chapter. The main point is: Don't attempt to use the categories of *knowledge, comprehension,* and *application* if they don't apply. In teaching how to play basketball, for example, don't use objectives like "Comprehends the rules of play" and "Applies the rules of play during a game." This implies a higher level of cognitive outcomes than the activity warrants. It is much better to state these outcomes as follows:

Knows the rules of play.

Follows the rules during a game.

Statements such as these indicate what the students are expected to be able to do, without implying there is some higher level of cognitive outcome involved. This illustrates why one should not become a slave to any particular classification system. Forcing statements of objectives to fit a certain set of categories has no advantage. The categories of knowledge, comprehension, and application should simply be guides for identifying possible objectives for a given area of instruction.

Adapting Statements to Levels of Instruction

Many intended learning outcomes are applicable to various levels of instruction. Common general instructional objectives that cut across grade levels can be adapted to a particular instructional level by means of the specific learning outcomes. For example, the objective "knows basic concepts" might vary from the lower primary level to the upper secondary levels (high school and college) as follows:

1. Knows basic concepts (lower primary level).
    1.1. Identifies a picture indicating relative position (e.g., first, last).
    1.2. Identifies a picture indicating relative size (e.g., biggest, smallest).
    1.3. Identifies a picture indicating relative amount (e.g., most, least).
    1.4. Identifies a picture indicating relative distance (e.g., farthest, nearest).

2. Knows basic concepts (upper secondary level).
    2.1. Describes the characteristics of the concept.
    2.2. Identifies the concept from a brief description of it.
    2.3. Identifies symbols representing the concept.
    2.4. Distinguishes between the concept and similar concepts.

At the lower primary level the type of performance accepted as evidence of achievement of the objective must, of course, be stated in simpler and more specific terms. However, as illustrated here, if carefully stated, such terms can clearly convey what primary students can do to demonstrate that they know basic concepts.

These examples, showing how the same instructional objectives can be used at different levels of instruction by adapting them through the specific learning outcomes, do not imply that it is always wise to do so. It is probably most useful where there is an attempt to focus on those common objectives in the areas of basic concepts and skills that are emphasized throughout the various grade levels. Even then, it is often advantageous to modify a general instructional objective to more closely fit the emphasis at a particular level of instruction and merely classify the objective as a knowledge outcome.

As with knowledge outcomes, comprehension and application objectives can be adapted to the level of instruction by means of the specific learning outcomes. For example, comprehension of a short story at the lower primary level and the secondary level might vary as follows:

1. Comprehends a short story (lower primary level).
    1.1. Describes what happened in the story.
    1.2. Chooses the most appropriate title for the story.
    1.3. Explains why the title is most appropriate.
    1.4. Explains why a particular event occurred in the story.
    1.5. Explains why the characters of the story acted as they did.

2. Comprehends a short story (secondary level).
    2.1. Describes the main theme of the story.
    2.2. Explains the significance of certain events in the story.
    2.3. Identifies similarities and differences between characters.
    2.4. States possible motivations for the actions of the characters.
    2.5. Describes what might happen next if the story were to be continued.

As noted earlier, there is no reason that comprehension outcomes must include the term *comprehension* in the statements of the general objectives. When writing objectives at the comprehension and application levels, you may want to use terminology that fits the subject more closely and describes student performance in more specific terms, as follows:

1. Translates from verbal to mathematical form (comprehension).
    1.1. Converts words to numerals.
    1.2. Converts words to mathematical symbols.
    1.3. Converts verbal statements to mathematical formulas.
    1.4. Writes an equation that represents a word problem.

2. Writes an effective paragraph (application).
    2.1. States a main idea.
    2.2. Relates sentences to the main idea.
    2.3. Uses complete sentences.
    2.4. Uses descriptive words to emphasize points.
    2.5. Arranges sentences in a meaningful sequence.
    2.6. Uses capitals and punctuation correctly.
    2.7. Spells words correctly.
    2.8. Follows grammar and usage conventions.

You can see from these examples that intended learning outcomes can be stated in various ways. The task is to state each general instructional objective and set of specific learning outcomes so that they most clearly describe student performance when the objectives have been achieved. Although knowledge, comprehension, and application outcomes are common to many areas of instruction, the outcomes must typically be adapted to a particular situation by variation in wording. Just be sure that the terminology selected is relevant to the area and level of instruction.

The Problem of Limiting Objectives to Intellectual Outcomes

Although we are focusing here on intellectual outcomes, recognize that affective or psychomotor elements are often present as well. Our earlier objective "Comprehends a short story," for example, focused on intellectual reactions to the story, but students also may have emotional reactions to the story. Did the story change how students felt toward the people or events in the story? Did the students empathize with some of the characters? Were the students interested or bored by the story? These and similar questions may suggest outcomes that are equally important in assessing students' reactions to short stories. Such outcomes can be stated separately or incorporated as part of a larger objective that includes both comprehension and affect, depending on the nature of the instruction.

Similarly, psychomotor activities focus on skills but typically include both cognitive and affective components. Even such a routine skill as setting up laboratory equipment requires knowledge about the equipment, skill in selecting and assembling it, and an attitude of care during the procedure. Whether these are listed as separate objectives or combined to reflect the integrated nature of the activity again depends on the nature of the instruction. Use separate objectives if they more clearly convey the intended learning outcomes, but don't separate them just so they can be classified as cognitive, affective, or psychomotor.

Summary

1. Most areas of instruction include knowledge outcomes (i.e., remembering material), comprehension outcomes (i.e., grasping the meaning of material), and application outcomes (i.e., using the information in some way).

2. All three levels may be concerned with terms, facts, rules, procedures, concepts, principles, or theories, but the higher levels—comprehension and application— require the use of some novelty (e.g., new interpretations, new problems, new contextual settings).

3. The terms *knowledge, comprehension,* and *application* can be used directly in the statements of general objectives, if they are appropriate to the instruction and can be defined by a list of specific learning outcomes that clarifies their meaning.

4. In some cases the categories of knowledge, comprehension, and application simply provide a framework that serves as a guide for identifying objectives that are then stated in more specific terms to fit a particular situation.

5. Some instructional objectives can be used for various areas and levels of instruction (e.g., "knows basic terms") by writing specific learning outcomes that are relevant to each particular situation.

6. Some instructional objectives can best be adapted to a particular area or level of instruction by restating both the general instructional objectives and the specific learning outcomes.

7. Avoid stating objectives at the higher cognitive levels if the intended learning outcomes require only knowledge and skills (e.g., keyboarding).

8. It is usually better to state cognitive, affective, and psychomotor outcomes separately, but if an intended learning outcome is most clearly stated by including more than one type of performance in the objective, don't modify it simply so that the objectives can be classified into separate categories.

Exercises

1. Select one of the content areas in Figure 6.1. Use the general examples of knowledge, comprehension, and application outcomes to write three general instructional objectives and associated specific learning outcomes for a lower primary class.

2. Select one of the content areas in Figure 6.1. Use the general examples of knowledge, comprehension, and application outcomes to write three general instructional objectives and associated specific learning outcomes for an upper secondary class.

Chapter 7

Writing Objectives for Higher-Level Thinking Skills

INSTRUCTIONAL OBJECTIVE:

Writes objectives for higher-level thinking skills.

1. Describes the characteristics of thinking skills at the analysis, synthesis, and evaluation levels.
2. Distinguishes between well-stated and poorly stated objectives at the thinking level.
3. Writes a thinking skill objective and set of specific learning outcomes that are useful with various units of study.
4. Writes a thinking skill objective and set of specific learning outcomes for a particular area and level of instruction.
5. Writes a general instructional objective and set of specific learning outcomes that include both cognitive and affective outcomes at the thinking level.

Thinking skills and strategies have been described in many different ways. Such terms as *critical thinking*, *creative thinking*, and *problem solving* are commonly used frameworks for classifying specific sets of thinking skills and strategies. Critical thinking skills emphasize analysis and evaluation (e.g., identifying and analyzing a problem and evaluating possible solutions). Creative thinking skills emphasize the production of something new (e.g., producing a plan for solving a problem). Although critical and creative thinking are frequently described separately in the literature, elements of both are usually involved in various types of problem solving. Thus in this chapter we shall be concerned with thinking skills in general and not limit them to a particular type of thinking.

Thinking strategies in problem solving typically include a sequence of activities such as (1) identifying and analyzing a problem, (2) applying past learning, (3) gathering new information, (4) organizing and comparing data, (5) analyzing elements and relationships, (6) clarifying and judging alternatives, and (7) summarizing a solution or selecting a course of action. Within this problem-solving process a number of specific thinking skills (e.g., ability to identify the adequacy of data) and affective behaviors (e.g., objectivity) are involved, as well as lower-level cognitive outcomes (e.g., knowledge of concepts) and general problem-solving strategies (e.g., observing, asking questions).

Figure 7.1 presents a collection of specific thinking skills at the levels of analysis, synthesis, and evaluation; these will provide you with flexibility in writing instructional objectives in the area of higher-level thinking. The examples make it possible to select a comprehensive list of specific skill outcomes when focusing on a major problem, or to select a few for a more limited use. Also, the vast array of specific skills in the collection provides for variation from one area to another. For example, analysis in science, social studies, English, mathematics, art, music, and vocational courses are likely to emphasize different specific skills because of the nature of the content or the types of problems to be solved. Similar differences will be found at the levels of synthesis and evaluation. Although the lists of specific thinking skills in Figure 7.1 are not exhaustive, they provide a good starting point for writing objectives in this important area.

Listing the array of specific thinking skills in Figure 7.1 separately does not imply that they should be taught and tested apart from course content. In some cases, a specific thinking skill (e.g., distinguishes between fact and opinion) might be tested and taught separately before it is applied to a particular problem involving analysis. But more commonly, the specific skills will be taught and tested in relation to particular problems or situations in a specific content area. As with other specific learning outcomes, the thinking skills describe how students are to respond, and the content area describes the types of situations and problems to which they are to respond.

The lists of specific outcomes in Figure 7.1 are confined to higher-level thinking skills at the analysis, synthesis, and evaluation levels. This means the following types of outcomes important to problem solving are not included:

1. Lower-level cognitive outcomes (knowledge, comprehension, application). These play an important role in the total thinking process but were covered in the last chapter.

2. General thinking strategies such as asking questions, observing, comparing, and organizing data.

3. Affective outcomes such as attitudes, curiosity, independent thought, honesty, objectivity, open-mindedness, perseverance, respect for evidence, and willingness to suspend judgment. Affective outcomes are an integral part of thinking but will be described later in the chapter.

In some cases it may be necessary to incorporate into a description of an objective involving thinking skill outcomes some elements of lower-level outcomes (e.g., interpretation), general thinking strategies (e.g., asks questions), or affective outcomes (e.g., curiosity). There is no attempt here to isolate them except as a basis for discussion and illustration.

Making a Useful List of Outcomes

Stating outcomes that are applicable to many types of content make them useful with different units or areas of instruction. The following lists, for example, will indicate how students are to perform when they demonstrate thinking skills in reading, evaluating an

Figure 7.1 Examples of Specific Thinking Skills

ANALYSIS

Identifies—

adequacy	contradictions	inconsistencies	reasoning
assumptions	criteria	inferences	relationships
attributes	defects	limitations	relevance
biases	distortions	main ideas	stereotypes
causes	effects	nature of evidence	superstition
central issues	elements	organization	trends
completeness	errors	plausibility	validity
concepts	exceptions	problems	variables
consequences	fallacies	procedures	

Distinguishes between—

accurate and inaccurate	facts and value statements
cause and effect	plausible and implausible
consistent and inconsistent	possible and probable
dominant and subordinate	relevant and irrelevant
essential and inessential	summaries and conclusions
facts and conclusions	supportive and contradictory
facts and hypotheses	valid and invalid
facts and inferences	verifiable and unverifiable
facts and opinions	warranted and unwarranted

Infers—

assumptions	characteristics	motives	purposes
attitudes	conditions	organization	qualities
biases	moods	points of view	relationships

SYNTHESIS

Formulates—

classification systems	generalizations	principles
concepts	hypotheses	problems
conclusions	musical compositions	questions
designs	plans	stories
equations	poetry	summaries
explanations	predictions	theories

EVALUATION

Generates—

criteria	standards	procedures

Judges—

accuracy	correctness	significance
adequacy	credibility	standards
appropriateness	organization	usefulness
clarity	reasonableness	validity
cohesiveness	reasoning	values
completeness	relationships	worth
consistency	reliability	

argument, or planning an experiment. The statements are general enough to be used with various types of reading and course material.

1. Demonstrates thinking skills in reading.
    1.1. Distinguishes between main ideas and supporting details.
    1.2. Distinguishes between facts and opinions.
    1.3. Distinguishes between facts and inferences.
    1.4. Identifies cause–effect relations.
    1.5. Identifies errors in reasoning.
    1.6. Distinguishes between valid and invalid conclusions.
    1.7. Identifies assumptions underlying conclusions.

2. Evaluates arguments for and against a proposal.
    2.1. Identifies the accuracy of statements.
    2.2. Identifies bias in statements.
    2.3. Distinguishes between relevant and irrelevant statements.
    2.4. Distinguishes between supportive and nonsupportive statements.
    2.5. Identifies the assumptions underlying an argument.
    2.6. Identifies the adequacy of an argument.
    2.7. Identifies the consistency of the facts supporting an argument.
    2.8. Identifies the credibility of sources cited in an argument.

3. Prepares a plan for an experiment.
    3.1. Identifies the problem to be solved.
    3.2. Formulates questions relevant to the problem.
    3.3. Formulates hypotheses in appropriate verbal or mathematical form.
    3.4. Describes controls for variables.
    3.5. Formulates experimental procedures.
    3.6. Formulates observation and measurement procedures.
    3.7. Describes the methods of data analysis.
    3.8. Describes how the results will be presented.

Other specific outcomes could be stated for these general objectives to make them more comprehensive and detailed, or to adapt them to a particular type of reading, experiment, or proposal. These lists, however, indicate the approximate amount of detail needed for clarifying what students can do when they have achieved these higher-level learning outcomes.

Adapting Statements to Areas of Instruction

Although you should try to write the statements of specific thinking skills so that they are applicable to various units of study, the statements still must be in harmony with the area of instruction in which they are used. You can do this by carefully selecting and writing the specific learning outcomes used to describe the general instructional objective. For example, the same general objective might be described in social studies and mathematics as follows:

1. Demonstrates ability to solve problems (social studies).
    1.1. Identifies the main idea in the problem.
    1.2. States the problem in question form.
    1.3. Selects relevant source materials.
    1.4. Analyzes source materials to obtain answers to the problem.
    1.5. Distinguishes between noncausal relations and cause–effect relations.
    1.6. Summarizes the findings from the source material.
    1.7. States conclusions that answer the problem question.

2. Demonstrates ability to solve problems (mathematics).
    2.1. Analyzes a word problem.
    2.2. Identifies the information relevant to solving the problem.
    2.3. Translates words into numerals and symbols.
    2.4. Formulates an equation that represents the problem.
    2.5. Estimates the approximate answer to the problem.
    2.6. Solves the equation to answer the problem.
    2.7. Verifies the problem answer using an alternate method.

The intended learning outcomes may, of course, be more closely adapted to a particular area of instruction by also modifying the general instructional objective. Here we are simply showing how a common instructional objective can be adapted by altering the specific types of student performance that represent the "ability to solve problems."

Adapting Statements to Levels of Instruction

As with lower-level cognitive outcomes, higher-level thinking objectives can be adapted to the various levels of instruction by (1) modifying the lists of specific learning outcomes, (2) varying the difficulty of the problem to be solved or the content to be evaluated, or (3) modifying both the general objective and the specific learning outcomes.

Instruction at the elementary level typically uses fewer and more simply stated specific learning outcomes to define an instructional objective. Thus, if we were to define the instructional objective in reading, illustrated earlier, we might prepare a list such as the following:

1. Demonstrates thinking skills in reading.
    1.1. Identifies the main ideas in a story.
    1.2. Distinguishes between stated details and implied information.
    1.3. Describes the sequence of events in the story.
    1.4. Tells why particular events happened in the story.

1.5. Describes why the characters acted as they did.

1.6. Summarizes the meaning of the story.

The earlier objective "Evaluates arguments for and against a proposal" provides an example of how the same objective and list of specific learning outcomes can be used at different levels of instruction by varying the difficulty of the problems or content to be evaluated. Relatively simple proposals can be selected for use at lower levels of instruction, and more complex proposals regarding social, economic, or political issues can be used at higher levels. Although the specific learning outcomes may need to be varied slightly to fit different instructional levels or issues, the specific learning outcomes listed earlier for this objective are widely adaptable.

With some modification and simplification of the specific learning outcomes listed for the objective "Prepares a plan for an experiment," it would be possible to use the objective at the elementary level. In some cases, however, it would be desirable to modify the general objective to indicate an experiment for a particular problem and to list the specific outcomes in terms of that problem as follows:

1. Designs an experiment to prove that a plant grows better in some soils than in others.

1.1. Predicts the type of soil in which plants grow best.

1.2. Describes each type of soil to be used.

1.3. Describes the factors to be considered in plant selection.

1.4. Lists the factors to be kept constant.

1.5. Describes the measurement procedures to be used.

1.6. Describes the procedural steps and length of the experiment.

1.7. Describes how the results will be presented.

Stating the objective and specific learning outcomes as specifically as this does not permit their use with other problems, although the general pattern of specific statements does provide a guiding framework. Also, when you state the experimental problem as part of the objective, the students, of course, are not given practice in problem identification.

Especially, when you simplify the statements take care not to reduce the student performance from a higher-level thinking skill to a lower-level routine activity. Tapping higher-level thinking requires problems or situations that are new to students. Problems they have already solved, or seen solved, are recall-level tasks.

Affective Components of Thinking

Thinking involves both cognitive and affective components. Until now we have limited our descriptions and illustrations of thinking outcomes to the cognitive area. Here we shall focus on the affective aspects of thinking. Although they are separated for discussion purposes, they are, of course, integrated in various ways in practice.

A collection of some of the more common types of specific affective behaviors associated with thinking skills are shown in Figure 7.2. These lists make it possible to select those that are most appropriate for a particular situation. In some cases they might be

Figure 7.2   Examples of Specific Affective Behaviors in Thinking

Demonstrates—
 care in observing   originality
 curiosity   perseverance
 independent thought   respect for evidence
 integrity   willingness to suspend judgment
 objectivity   willingness to revise opinions
 open-mindedness

Disposition to seek—
 alternative answers   natural causes
 confirming data   reasons for events
 contrary points of view   relevant information
 credible sources   verifiable facts

Appreciates importance of—
 a clearly stated problem   social consequences of findings
 care in observation   persistence
 commitment to the task   preciseness of results
 extending effort   questioning of results
 orderly procedures   verification of results
 sampling effect on findings   viewpoints of others

included as part of a separate objective concerned with attitudes or dispositions that support thinking skills, as illustrated by "displays a scientific attitude" in Chapter 8. In other cases, as illustrated in this section, they might be included along with cognitive components in describing the application of thinking skills to some content area or some type of problem solving. As with the cognitive components of thinking, a particular objective may include relatively few affective behaviors or a large number, depending on the nature of the objective, the level of instruction, and the type of problem or situation.

In defining the application of thinking skills to the solution of problems, the cognitive components and affective components can become closely integrated, resulting in a list of specific outcomes as follows:

1. Applies thinking skills in solving social problems.
 1.1. Identifies a common social problem.
 1.2. Analyzes the problem and related issues.
 1.3. States the problem and issues clearly.
 1.4. Gathers relevant information from credible sources.
 1.5. Distinguishes between facts and opinions.
 1.6. Identifies bias and other distortions in statements.
 1.7. Seeks viewpoints of others on the problem.
 1.8. Suspends judgment until information is complete.

    1.9. Identifies factors causing and contributing to the problem.

    1.10. Describes possible solutions to the problem.

    1.11. Describes the need for social action.

Note that although an attempt was made to define this objective in performance terms, affective elements pervade the statements. We can infer from the statements, for example, that the importance of a clearly stated problem is recognized (1.3), that there is a disposition to seek relevant information and use credible sources (1.4), that objectivity is being sought (1.5 and 1.6), that the viewpoints of others (1.7) and suspending judgment (1.8) are considered important, and that there is a disposition to seek causes (1.9) before obtaining solutions to a problem. Your inferences concerning these affective outcomes will, of course, require more than this one sample of behavior before they can be accepted as evidence of consistent tendencies or dispositions. All we are attempting to do here is to illustrate how you might include affective outcomes when you define thinking skills in problem solving.

Summary

1. Higher-level thinking skills are commonly discussed in the literature under such headings as critical thinking, creative thinking, and problem solving.

2. A learning outcome in a particular area may involve elements from different types of thinking (e.g., both critical and creative).

3. A list of specific thinking skills at the analysis, synthesis, and evaluation levels provides a basis for combining the skills in various ways to fit a particular problem or situation.

4. Be flexible when writing objectives at the thinking level. Avoid describing thinking as a fixed set of skills and strategies.

5. Instructional objectives at the thinking level require that the problems or situations be new to the students.

6. Write instructional objectives that are in general enough terms that they can be used with various units of study.

7. Adapt general thinking objectives to different areas or levels of instruction by modifying the list of specific skill outcomes, or modifying both the general objectives and the specific outcomes.

8. When writing instructional objectives at the thinking level, don't neglect the affective components of thinking. These might be stated as a separate objective (e.g., "displays a scientific attitude") or might be combined with cognitive elements.

Exercises

1. Write a generic thinking skills general instructional objective and specific learning outcomes useful with various units of study.

2. Write at least three versions of your general instructional objective (from Exercise 1), each for a particular unit of study and grade level. Specify the unit and grade level.

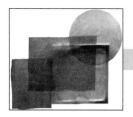

Chapter 8

Writing Objectives for Affective Outcomes

INSTRUCTIONAL OBJECTIVE:

Writes objectives for affective outcomes.

1. Describes the factors that make writing affective objectives so difficult.
2. Distinguishes between well-stated and poorly stated affective objectives.
3. Writes sample specific learning outcomes in the affective area that reflect observable behavior and those that reflect inner feelings only.
4. Writes an affective instructional objective and set of specific learning outcomes for a particular area and level of instruction.
5. Describes why it might be necessary to consider the types of assessment to be made when writing affective objectives.

Preparing intended learning outcomes is more difficult in the affective area than in the cognitive area for a number of reasons. First, the terminology used in this area is vague. Affective outcomes are concerned with feelings and emotions that are described by an individual's disposition, willingness, preferences, enjoyments, and similar terms that have a wide range of meanings and are difficult to describe in performance terms. Second, although some of the intended outcomes can be stated overtly (e.g., "asks questions"), others are covert and can only be inferred (e.g., "feels confident"). In the latter case, all we can do is state the types of behavior that best support the presence of the inferred characteristic. Third, affective outcomes are described in so many ways. In the literature they are typically classified under such headings as attitudes, interests, appreciations, and adjustments.

The affective domain of the *Taxonomy of Educational Objectives* (Krathwohl, Bloom, & Masia, 1964, see Appendix B.2), on the other hand, cuts across these categories and describes behavior within them, ranging from simple responses to complex behavior patterns. An "interest" response, for example, may vary from a person being simply aware that an activity exists to a strong preference for engaging in it. Fourth, as affective behaviors move from simple to complex, as in the *Taxonomy*, they become increasingly internalized and integrated with other behaviors (both affective and cognitive) to form complex value systems and behavior patterns. Thus, at higher levels it is more difficult to isolate and state intended learning outcomes in specific terms without destroying their integrated nature. Also, at higher levels overt responses are less dependable as evidence of internal states. For example, individuals may feel insecure but act completely confident.

Basing Statements on the *Taxonomy* Categories

One way to start is to review the categories in the affective domain of the *Taxonomy* and use these categories as a guide. This procedure might result in statements such as the following:

1. Participates in classroom activities (receiving and responding).
   1.1. Listens attentively.
   1.2. Asks relevant questions.
   1.3. Participates in classroom discussion.
   1.4. Volunteers for special tasks.
   1.5. Contributes material for the bulletin board.
   1.6. Helps others when requested.

2. Shows concern for the welfare of others (valuing).
   2.1. Asks others if they need help.
   2.2. Helps others with their problems.
   2.3. Shares materials with others.
   2.4. Encourages others to do well.
   2.5. Meets obligations in doing group work.
   2.6. Assists those reluctant to participate in group work.
   2.7. Obtains permission before using others' materials.
   2.8. Thanks and commends others, when appropriate.

3. Formulates a rationale concerning the role of society in conserving natural resources (organization).
   3.1. Relates the needs of society to the conservation of resources.
   3.2. Describes the probable effects on society if resources are wantonly used.
   3.3. Describes the probable effects on society if the use of resources is overly restricted.
   3.4. States personal position reflecting a reasonable balance between the needs of society and the needs to conserve resources.

4. Respects the scientific process (characterization).
   4.1. Favors evidence that results from scientific studies.

   4.2. Seeks objectivity in the interpretation of evidence.

   4.3. Changes opinions when evidence is contrary to beliefs.

   4.4. Suspends judgment when evidence is inadequate.

   4.5. Shows skepticism when statements are unsupported.

   4.6. Questions evidence derived from inadequate studies.

   4.7. Bases ideas and opinions on the best scientific evidence available.

These examples illustrate some of the difficulties mentioned earlier in stating affective outcomes. At the lower levels, the specific learning outcomes can be more easily stated in terms of overt behavior that can be observed by the teacher. At the higher levels, where the desired behavior becomes more internalized and integrated, the descriptive terminology becomes more vague and refers to feelings and attitudes. This typically requires assessment by means of self-report methods and other techniques for getting at an individual's internal state.

Basing Statements on Traditional Categories

Because affective outcomes are typically described in the literature under the categories of attitudes, interests, appreciations, and adjustments, some teachers prefer to state objectives using these frameworks. When this is done, the *Taxonomy* can still be useful by helping in the statement of specific learning outcomes. With our two-step method of defining intended learning outcomes, a general instructional objective (e.g., "shows interest in reading") may be useful at different levels of instruction, but the specific learning outcomes clarify the types of performance expected at a particular level.

Attitudes are probably the most common affective outcome stressed by teachers. Although the major emphasis in teaching may be on cognitive outcomes or skill learning, most teachers want their students to develop a favorable attitude toward their area of instruction and toward learning in general. In addition, other attitude outcomes may constitute an important component of the course. In science courses, for example, the development of a scientific attitude is typically a major objective of the instruction. The following example illustrates how this objective might be defined by a list of specific learning outcomes:

1. Displays a scientific attitude.

   1.1. Demonstrates curiosity in identifying problems.

   1.2. Seeks natural causes of events.

   1.3. Demonstrates open-mindedness when seeking answers.

   1.4. Suspends judgment until all evidence is available.

   1.5. Respects evidence from credible sources.

   1.6. Shows objectivity in analyzing evidence and drawing conclusions.

   1.7. Seeks ways to verify results.

   1.8. Shows willingness to revise conclusions as new evidence becomes available.

The following statements of intended learning outcomes illustrate how objectives might be written for other traditional categories found in the literature:

2. Demonstrates interest in mathematics.
   2.1. Asks questions that indicate curiosity about math.
   2.2. Asks for extra problems to solve.
   2.3. Completes assignments on time.
   2.4. Brings examples of math problems to class.
   2.5. Helps others with math problems.
   2.6. Seeks ways to improve math learning.
   2.7. Uses math in out-of-school activities.
   2.8. Asks about careers in math.

3. Appreciates good literature.
   3.1. Describes the differences between good and poor literature.
   3.2. Distinguishes between selections of good and poor literature.
   3.3. States reasons for classifying a selection as good or poor.
   3.4. Selects and reads good literature during free-reading period.
   3.5. Explains why he/she likes the selections that are read.
   3.6. Describes his/her emotional reactions to the selections.
   3.7. Expresses a desire for more time to read good literature.

4. Demonstrates good social adjustment.
   4.1. Interacts harmoniously with others.
   4.2. Shares ideas with others.
   4.3. Confines classroom discussions to the issues.
   4.4. Shows concern for the needs and feelings of others.
   4.5. Is selected by others for group activities.
   4.6. Cooperates with others in carrying out activities.
   4.7. Is trustworthy in dealing with others.
   4.8. Is courteous and considerate in working with others.

Of course, many other types of objectives could be listed here. All we are attempting to do is illustrate the various ways that objectives might be stated and defined in the affective area.

In some cases it might be necessary for you to consider the types of assessment to be made when writing objectives. If observations are to be the main method of evaluating the intended outcomes (e.g., using rating scales or checklists), then it will be necessary to attempt to state the specific outcomes in terms of overt behavior only. If self-report instruments are to be used (e.g., attitude scales and interest inventories), then the statements can include more emphasis on feelings, opinions, preferences, and other internal states. For some types of outcomes both methods of assessment may be appropriate.

Adapting Statements to Areas and Levels of Instruction

As with other types of intended learning outcomes, affective objectives can be adapted to various areas and levels of instruction by selecting specific learning outcomes that best describe the objective in a particular situation. For example, a common objective like "Demonstrates a positive attitude toward learning" can be adapted as follows:

1. Demonstrates a positive attitude toward learning (elementary math).
    1.1. Pays attention when problems are explained.
    1.2. Follows directions when solving problems.
    1.3. Works independently when solving problems.
    1.4. Asks questions when a procedure is not clear.
    1.5. Completes class assignments on time.

2. Demonstrates a positive attitude toward learning (secondary English).
    2.1. Listens attentively during class discussions.
    2.2. Asks questions and makes comments that show interest.
    2.3. Participates eagerly in reading and writing projects.
    2.4. Uses the dictionary whenever needed.
    2.5. Works independently on assigned projects.
    2.6. Completes homework assignments on time.
    2.7. Willingly accepts teacher's criticisms and suggestions on assigned projects.

These sample objectives are, of course, merely intended as illustrations of how to adapt the same objective to a particular situation and do not imply that affective objectives should be stated in a standard way. Sometimes you will need to modify both the general objective and the specific learning outcomes.

Deciding if Affective Outcomes Should be Stated Separately

In some cases it may be wise to state the affective outcomes separately, as has been illustrated. In others they may be most effective if combined with objectives describing a cognitive or skill outcome. The following objective for safety in using laboratory equipment illustrates a separate objective that might be better combined with a skill statement concerning the use of laboratory equipment:

1. Uses laboratory equipment in a safe manner.
    1.1. Examines equipment before using.
    1.2. Wears appropriate safety gear.
    1.3. Uses care in setting up equipment.

    1.4. Follows safe procedures in using equipment.

    1.5. Dismantles equipment carefully.

    1.6. Cleans and restores equipment when done.

Although each specific learning outcome focuses on safety, most of them also include procedural skills. Thus, by adding a few others concerning the assembling and manipulating of the equipment, you could have a general objective on use of the equipment. On the other hand, if various types of equipment were being used and you wanted to emphasize safety, the separate objective would be the better choice. Where the use of equipment or machinery is dangerous, you will want to stress safety in your objectives, your teaching, and your assessment. It is your instructional intent that should help you decide whether to prepare separate statements of affective outcomes or combine them with cognitive or skill outcomes.

Summary

1. Objectives in the affective area are more difficult to write than cognitive and skill outcomes because of the vagueness of terminology, the need to infer covert behavior (e.g., feelings) from observed actions or self-report, and the various ways affective outcomes are classified. In some cases, affective outcomes are best stated as an integral part of cognitive and skill outcomes.

2. Affective objectives can be written in many different ways using various categories as a framework.

3. Write affective objectives in terms of observable behavior whenever possible, but don't neglect feelings, opinions, and preferences if important.

4. Consider the assessment procedure to be used when writing affective objectives. Overt behavior is assessed by observation techniques (e.g., rating scales and checklists) and covert by self-report instruments (e.g., attitude scales and interest inventories).

5. Use terminology as precise as possible when writing affective objectives, but don't neglect important outcomes just because they cannot be stated in precise terms.

6. Adapt affective objectives to the area and level of instruction by modifying the specific outcomes.

7. Affective objectives may be written separately or combined with cognitive or skill objectives. The choice should be guided by which method best conveys your instructional intent.

Exercises

1. Why is it hard to write good instructional objectives for affective outcomes?

2. Brainstorm as many specific learning outcomes as you can for the general instructional objective, "Shows interest in reading." Write as many as you can think

of; don't limit them to a good single set of specific learning outcomes for one class.

3. Use the specific learning outcomes you wrote for Exercise 2 to do the following things.

   a. First, identify any you think are of poor quality and tell why. Then remove them from the set.

   b. Use the remaining specific learning outcomes on your list to write two good instructional objectives about showing an interest in reading, one for a lower primary reading class and one for an upper secondary English class.

Chapter 9

Writing Performance Objectives for Skills and Products

INSTRUCTIONAL OBJECTIVE:

Writes performance objectives for skills and products.

1. Describes the importance of considering performance skills when writing instructional objectives.
2. Writes an objective and set of specific performance outcomes that focus on a procedure.
3. Writes an objective and set of specific performance outcomes that focus on a product.
4. Writes objectives and sets of specific performance outcomes that focus on both procedure and product.

Instructional outcomes concerned with performance skills play an important role in education. At the primary level, performance outcomes include such things as speaking, handwriting, reading aloud, drawing, and singing. At the higher levels of instruction, performance outcomes include laboratory skills, communication skills, and various specialized performance skills in agriculture, art, business, home economics, industrial education, music, and physical education. In recent years, instructional outcomes have also focused on problem-solving performance in all areas of study, as a means of integrating learning and applying it to problems like those in the "real world."

In this chapter, we are concerned with how to state the more traditional objectives for performance skills and products. Chapter 10 will be concerned with stating performance objectives for problem-solving projects. In both chapters, our sample objectives and lists of specific performance outcomes are best viewed as models or guides. They illustrate the procedure for stating performance outcomes, but they are stated in broad terms. You may need to modify them to fit a particular situation.

Despite the significance of performance skills as valued learning outcomes, teachers have sometimes neglected them in the past when writing objectives and planning for the assessment of student learning. This is due, at least in part, to the difficulty and time-consuming nature of performance assessment and the subjectivity in judging performance skills. Although performance assessment is a difficult task, it can be made easier by clearly specifying the intended outcomes. The specific performance outcomes can then serve as criteria for scoring or judging student performance. Clearly stated performance outcomes also can contribute to student learning by communicating to students what is involved in an effective performance, and by providing guidelines for self-assessment of learning progress. Self-assessment is important in developing independent performers.

When you prepare objectives in this area, you may focus on either:

1. The procedures or process during the performance
2. The product resulting from the performance
3. Both the procedures and the product

In giving a speech, for example, the performance itself is important. In writing a research report, however, the product is the focus of attention. In some areas, such as keyboarding, emphasis is given to both the procedures (e.g., use of the touch system and the word-processing program) and the product (e.g., error-free letters). We shall describe and illustrate how to write objectives in each of the three areas.

Writing Objectives for Procedure Outcomes

In stating and defining performance objectives, the focus should be on the performance itself (e.g., process) when:

1. The act of performing is the main outcome, or there is no product.
2. A diagnosis of the performance is needed to improve learning.
3. The performance is based on a collection of elements or series of steps that can be identified.

For any particular performance there are a number of elements, or procedures, that are crucial to a successful performance. Thus in writing objectives in this area you should analyze the performance to identify those elements or procedural steps that define a satisfactory performance. These are then listed as specific learning outcomes under the general objective as follows:

1. Presents an oral report to the class.
    1.1. States the topic at the beginning of the report.
    1.2. Speaks clearly and loudly enough to be heard.
    1.3. Uses language appropriate for the report.
    1.4. Uses correct grammar.
    1.5. Speaks at a satisfactory rate.

1.6. Looks at the class members when speaking.

1.7. Uses natural movements and appears relaxed.

1.8. Presents the material in an organized manner.

1.9. Holds the interest of the class.

[Note that this procedural objective would probably be used in conjunction with a cognitive objective about the quality of the report's content.]

2. Uses laboratory equipment properly (science).

   2.1. Selects appropriate equipment for an experiment.

   2.2. Assembles equipment correctly for the experiment.

   2.3. Manipulates equipment as needed during the experiment.

   2.4. Measures accurately with proper measuring device.

   2.5. Follows safety rules in conducting experiment.

   2.6. Uses materials without wasting any.

   2.7. Completes experiment within time limits.

   2.8. Cleans equipment and returns to proper place.

3. Applies varnish correctly.

   3.1. Sands and prepares surface properly.

   3.2. Wipes dust from surface with appropriate cloth.

   3.3. Selects appropriate brush.

   3.4. Selects varnish and checks varnish flow.

   3.5. Pours needed amount of varnish into clean container.

   3.6. Puts brush properly into varnish (one-third of bristle length).

   3.7. Wipes excess varnish from brush on inside edge of container.

   3.8. Applies varnish to surface with smooth strokes.

   3.9. Works from center of surface toward the edges.

   3.10. Brushes with the grain of the wood.

   3.11. Uses light strokes to smooth the varnish.

   3.12. Checks surface for completeness.

   3.13. Cleans brush with appropriate cleaner.

   3.14. Does *not* pour excess varnish back into can.

   3.15. Cleans work area.

As you review these objectives, note that in some cases the order of the specific learning outcomes is not especially important (e.g., oral presentation), whereas in others they define a systematic, step-by-step procedure (e.g., the application of varnish). Where order of procedure is significant in the performance, place the outcomes in the proper order under the objective. This will make it easier to judge the performance and to detect errors.

When specific learning outcomes are properly stated, they can be easily converted to a checklist by simply adding a place to check "yes" or "no" for each procedure, or to a rating scale by adding a place to rate each procedure as it is performed. These instruments can be used both to guide student learning and to evaluate performance. Thus when writing the list of specific learning outcomes, use language that students can understand easily and that will provide clear statements for checking or rating learning progress.

Writing Objectives for Product Outcomes

Performance objectives should focus on the product resulting from the performance when:

1. The product is the main outcome of the performance.
2. The product has identifiable characteristics that can be used in evaluating the quality of the product.
3. Considerable variation exists in the procedures that can be used in producing the product, or the procedures are not observable to the instructor (e.g., out-of-class work).

If the objective indicates a product and the characteristics of the product can be identified and clearly defined, the specific learning outcomes are stated as criteria that describe a satisfactory product as follows:

1. Constructs a bar graph.
    1.1. Uses a separate bar for each measure.
    1.2. Matches length of each bar to data.
    1.3. Arranges bars in some logical order.
    1.4. Makes bars wider than spaces between them.
    1.5. Uses scale and guidelines that make bars easy to interpret.
    1.6. Identifies each bar with a label.
    1.7. Uses title that clearly indicates the nature of the graph.

2. Writes an effective composition.
    2.1. Expresses ideas clearly.
    2.2. Uses ideas that are logical.
    2.3. Relates ideas to the main thesis.
    2.4. Organizes the thesis to fit the topic.
    2.5. Writes well-structured, relevant paragraphs.
    2.6. Uses words that effectively convey meaning.
    2.7. Observes grammar and usage conventions.

As with procedure outcomes, the list of specific statements defining a product can be easily converted to a checklist or rating scale for use in performance assessment. Keep the statements simple and clear so that the assessment instrument can be used by students, both as a guide to learning and as a basis for self-evaluation.

In addition to being important in general education, products are important in many specialized areas. Courses in art, business, family and consumer sciences, and industrial education include products that are highly valued as learning outcomes. In most of these areas, however, both the procedures and the product are to be included when defining performance objectives.

Focusing on Both Procedure and Product Outcomes

Performance objectives should include both procedure and product outcomes when:

1. A clear set of procedures exists for producing the product (e.g., cooking recipe, steps in a woodworking project).
2. Learning is at an early stage and the product can be improved by correcting procedural errors.
3. Both the process and the product have identifiable elements that can be described and observed.

Most performance objectives in the school are concerned with entry-level performance. The aim is to learn the proper procedures and to obtain a *satisfactory* level of performance, rather than a high degree of proficiency (unless it's a trade or professional school). Thus, wherever feasible, you should direct your focus toward both the procedures used and the product. By adequately describing the procedures, we can provide guidelines for diagnosing and improving those elements of the performance that will result in a better product. Our description of the product provides a means for evaluating the effect of the improved procedures on the quality of the product and the level of proficiency attained.

A generalized set of specific outcomes for the procedures and product of a woodworking project might be stated as follows:

1. Follows proper procedures.
    1.1. Follows the steps listed in the project plan.
    1.2. Selects appropriate materials to use.
    1.3. Selects proper tools for project.
    1.4. Uses tools correctly for each task.
    1.5. Works carefully to avoid waste of materials.
    1.6. Uses time efficiently and completes project on schedule.

2. Constructs a satisfactory product.
    2.1. Dimensions of product match specifications.
    2.2. Overall appearance reflects care in construction.
    2.3. Finish is even and of high quality.
    2.4. Joints are smooth and fit tightly.
    2.5. Parts (e.g., drawers) fit properly and function well.

These outcomes are stated in general enough terms that they would fit various woodworking projects. When stating outcomes for a particular project, you could, of course, state them in more specific terms.

In some cases, the process and product can be included in the same list of performance outcomes, as follows:

1. Corrects malfunction in electronic equipment.

    1.1. Selects appropriate tools and testing equipment.

    1.2. Applies steps in sequential order.

    1.3. Locates malfunctioning unit.

    1.4. Repairs or replaces malfunctioning unit.

    1.5. Tests equipment for proper functioning.

    1.6. Completes task in reasonable time.

    1.7. Follows safety procedures.

Although the product (i.e., properly functioning equipment) is the main goal, from an instructional standpoint the process is the focus of the performance task. We are assuming, of course, that the testing of the repaired equipment, as important as it is, plays a minor role. If not, you may want to use separate lists of performance outcomes for correcting the malfunction and for testing the repaired equipment. In other cases, you may also want to include a separate list for diagnosing the problem and for following safety procedures. How the intended learning outcomes are organized and stated depends to a large extent on the type and complexity of the performance and on your instructional intent.

In any event, where both procedure and product are important, the performance outcomes should be stated in the manner that is most useful for instruction and performance assessment. This may involve stating them in different ways to determine which method is best.

Isolating Performance Skills When Writing Objectives

Many types of performance include a combination of cognitive, affective, and skill outcomes (e.g., laboratory work and computer operation). In some cases, it may be desirable to break the performance down into each major type of outcome. For example, laboratory performance could be broken down into three separate objectives, as follows:

Knows laboratory procedures (cognitive).

Demonstrates skill in laboratory work (psychomotor).

Demonstrates a scientific attitude when writing and interpreting laboratory results (affective).

With statements such as these, you can describe and assess laboratory work by focusing on each of the three areas. The students' knowledge of procedures can be assessed by testing and observation, the demonstration of skill by a rating of performance, and the scientific attitude by observation, questioning, and examination of the laboratory reports. Such a breakdown lets you isolate each type of outcome for assessment purposes even though they might be integrated during the instruction.

In other instances, breaking an intended outcome down into separate categories might destroy the integrated nature of the performance. In giving a campaign speech, for example, the content of the speech, the stage presence and gestures used, and the attitudes reflected in the content and delivery of the speech are all part of the effectiveness of the speech and must be assessed as an integrated whole. Although judgments about the content, delivery, and attitudes can be made separately after the speech has been given, they cannot be made apart from any particular speech. In these cases, the intended outcomes should be stated in such a way that they reflect the integrated nature of the activity. They should not be broken down into separate categories just so the statements can be classified as cognitive, psychomotor, or affective.

Guidelines for Writing and Using Performance Objectives for Skills and Products

Although performance outcomes can be stated in many ways, the following guidelines focus on some of the important factors to keep in mind.

1. *Write each general objective so that it focuses on an important procedural skill or product.* The number of objectives will, of course, depend on the nature of the instruction. A simple skill may require only one general objective, whereas a complex performance skill may require several. Each objective should be able to be defined by a limited number of specific performance outcomes.

2. *Write specific performance outcomes that include the most important elements in the performance.* Focus on outcomes that are necessary for successfully demonstrating the performance skill. Don't include peripheral elements that may be present during the conduct of the performance but are not crucial to a successful completion of the task.

3. *Use a sufficient number of specific performance outcomes for each objective to clarify what students can do to demonstrate successful performance.* This means listing enough specific outcomes to define effective performance, but not so many that the observation and judgment of performance becomes burdensome.

4. *State the specific performance outcomes so they can serve as criteria for judging the performance.* This means focusing on observable aspects of the performance rather than on covert, unobservable behavior. For example, use "follows safety procedures," not "is safety conscious."

5. *State the specific performance outcomes in terms the students can understand.* If the statements are to provide students with a clear conception of what constitutes successful performance, they must be understood by students.

6. *Share the lists of performance outcomes with students before instruction begins.* This will provide students with a guide for directing their own learning, assessing their own learning progress, and, thus, moving them in the direction of more independent learning—all important aspects of skill development.

Summary

1. Performance objectives are important in most areas of learning but are frequently neglected, due in part to the difficulty and time-consuming nature of performance assessment and the subjectivity in judging performance skills.

2. Performance objectives can focus on the procedure, the product, or both the procedure and the product.

3. When performance objectives are clearly defined, the list of specific performance outcomes can be easily converted to checklists or rating scales for use in the assessment.

4. Performance objectives focusing on procedure should include all specific outcomes that are crucial to a successful performance.

5. When sequence of procedural steps is important, the steps should be listed in proper order.

6. Performance objectives focusing on a product should include characteristics that define a satisfactory product.

7. When performance objectives include both procedure and product, each should be defined by specific performance outcomes.

8. When writing performance objectives, isolate the skill element for descriptive and assessment purposes unless doing so destroys the integrated nature of the activity.

9. Guidelines for writing and using performance objectives for skills and products include writing general objectives that focus on important types of performance and defining each with lists of specific performance outcomes that:

   a. Include the important aspects of the skill or product.

   b. Are sufficient to describe successful performance.

   c. Are stated as criteria for judging the performance.

   d. Are stated in terms students can understand.

   e. Are shared with students before instruction begins.

Exercises

For each of the following exercises, select a topic and grade level you are interested in teaching.

1. Write a general instructional objective and set of specific performance outcomes that focus on a procedure.

2. Write a general instructional objective and set of specific performance outcomes that focus on a product.

3. Write a general instructional objective and set of specific performance outcomes that focus on a procedure and a product.

Chapter 10

Writing Performance Objectives for Problem-Solving Projects

INSTRUCTIONAL OBJECTIVE:

Writes performance objectives for problem-solving projects.

1. Describes the advantages of using problem-solving projects.
2. Distinguishes between restricted and extended problem-solving projects.
3. Writes performance objectives for a restricted performance project.
4. Writes performance objectives for an extended performance project.
5. Lists guidelines for writing and using performance objectives for problem-solving projects.

Instructional objectives for problem solving are concerned with knowledge, thinking skills, procedures, strategies, and a host of support skills (e.g., research skills, communication skills). This makes the identification and statement of objectives more difficult than in those areas limited to a specific skill or cognitive outcome (e.g., comprehension). The procedure is more manageable if the objectives are stated separately for *restricted* problem-solving projects and *extended* problem-solving projects.

Stating Objectives for Restricted Problem-Solving Projects

Restricted problem-solving projects are limited in scope, highly structured, and typically assigned by the teacher. They can be used in all subject areas, vary from simple to complex, stress the integration and application of learning to realistic-type problems, and provide opportunities for developing higher-level thinking skills. The following examples illustrate the nature of objectives for restricted problem-solving projects.

1. Write a proposal for solving a scientific problem.
   1.1. Describes the nature of the problem.
   1.2. Identifies the scientific concepts and principles involved.
   1.3. Analyzes and interprets relevant source material.
   1.4. Describes a plan for solving the problem.
   1.5. Lists the difficulties involved in carrying out the plan.
   1.6. Predicts the probable effects resulting from the proposed solution.

2. Describes an experiment for comparing two products.
   2.1. Describes the need that the products are designed to meet.
   2.2. Describes a means of testing and comparing the two products.
   2.3. Justifies the procedures used in the testing.
   2.4. Describes the results of the test.
   2.5. Writes recommendations concerning use of the two products.

3. Devises a method for predicting the outcome of an action or event.
   3.1. Describes the action or event.
   3.2. Describes the procedures to be used.
   3.3. Tries out the procedures.
   3.4. Analyzes and interprets the results.
   3.5. Revises the method, as needed.

4. Devises a measurement system using mathematical concepts.
   4.1. Describes the measurement problem.
   4.2. Devises the method of measurement.
   4.3. Explains the system using mathematical concepts.
   4.4. Summarizes the procedure in a mathematical formula.
   4.5. Tests the procedure and describes the results.

These objectives and specific performance outcomes are broadly stated and best serve as templates or models. You can adapt them to a specific area and level of instruction by naming the scientific problem (e.g., reduce smog), the two products (e.g., types of paper towels), the action or event (e.g., basketball game), or the measurement problem (e.g., the height of a tall tree) and modifying the specific performance outcomes as needed. Other examples of objectives for problem solving with restricted performance tasks can be found in Chapter 7.

Stating Objectives for Extended Problem-Solving Projects

Extended problem-solving projects are typically designed to enable students to deal with comprehensive, "real-world" problems that are poorly structured, have many possible solutions, and require an integration of many types of learning and skill. With an extended

Figure 10.1   Problem-Solving Skill Areas

Following are some of the major skill areas involved in problem-solving projects. They can either be incorporated into the objectives for problem-solving projects, or stated as separate objectives if that seems more desirable. In any event, they should be considered when planning for problem-solving projects.

thinking skills
research skills
resource locating skills
writing skills
display-making skills
group-work skills
speaking skills
self-assessment skills

problem-solving type of research project, the students are expected to identify and select the problem, design and carry out the study, write a report of the procedure and findings, design an experiment or construct display materials (e.g., model), and present and defend the study before the class or other groups. The performance objectives for the project may be presented to the students or developed cooperatively with them. The criteria for assessing the project are derived directly from the intended performance outcomes and are shared with students before beginning the projects.

Although some schools base the entire curriculum on a problem-solving approach, extended research projects are also used in a more traditional school curriculum. They are especially useful for developing a variety of performance skills that contribute to independent learning (see Figure 10.1).

The following sample objectives and specific performance outcomes illustrate the types of performance that can serve as a basis for assessing an extended research project, using a written report only.

1. Selects and states a realistic research problem.
    1.1. Lists a number of possible "real-world" problems on which to work.
    1.2. Selects a problem that is solvable.
    1.3. Selects a problem that is appropriate for his or her educational background.
    1.4. States the problem clearly and objectively.

2. Locates and selects relevant resources.
    2.1. Uses a variety of resources.
    2.2. Selects resource material that is most pertinent.
    2.3. Includes sufficient resource material to draw conclusions.

3. Writes a report describing the project.
    3.1. Describes the problem and nature of the study.
    3.2. Describes the study procedures used.

   3.3. Analyzes, synthesizes, and interprets the findings.

   3.4. Describes possible alternative interpretations of findings.

   3.5. States conclusions that are supported by the findings.

   3.6. Describes the limitations of the study.

   3.7. Lists suggestions for further study.

In some cases a research project is limited to a written report only, as in the previous list. In others, the written report simply provides a background for an experimental study, or it serves as a basis for designing a model, poster, or some other display material. In still other cases, the project is also presented orally to the class and through questioning the student defends the procedures and findings. These more comprehensive projects, of course, require the statement of additional performance outcomes.

The following sample objectives are broadly stated, but illustrate the general nature of the performance outcomes that might be stated for other aspects of a comprehensive research project.

1. Conducts an experimental study.

   1.1. Devises appropriate experimental procedures.

   1.2. Devises controls for variables in the study.

   1.3. Selects and manipulates needed equipment.

   1.4. Uses measurement procedures correctly.

   1.5. Analyzes and interprets the results.

   1.6. Formulates valid conclusions.

2. Prepares display material for the research project.

   2.1. Selects appropriate type of display (e.g., chart, graph, poster, model).

   2.2. Constructs a display that meets criteria for the type of display used.

   2.3. Constructs a display that is relevant to the findings of the research project.

   2.4. Constructs a display that summarizes and clarifies the findings of the research project.

3. Presents and defends the research project before a group.

   3.1. Describes the project in a well-organized manner.

   3.2. Summarizes the findings and their implications.

   3.3. Uses display materials to clarify ideas and relationships.

   3.4. Answers group members' questions directly and completely.

   3.5. Presents a report that reflects careful planning.

   3.6. Displays sound reasoning ability through presentation and answers to questions.

Extended research projects may be carried out individually by students or cooperatively in groups. In the latter case, performance outcomes should be stated in terms of how well an individual functioned in the group. For example, you might write statements such as the following:

1. Functions effectively in group work.
    1.1. Participates in the group discussions.
    1.2. Makes comments that are clear, well organized, and relevant.
    1.3. Asks meaningful questions.
    1.4. Listens attentively to the ideas of others.
    1.5. Asks questions and makes comments that reflect thought.
    1.6. Shows respect for other group members.
    1.7. Completes work assigned by group on schedule.

As with the illustrative objectives for the restricted problem-solving projects, these lists of performance outcomes are broadly stated to cover many types of extended problem-solving projects. Thus, they illustrate how to state the performance outcomes, but can best serve as models for stating outcomes that are more specific and relevant to your instructional area.

Guidelines for Writing and Using Performance Objectives in Problem-Solving Projects

If the purpose of problem-solving projects is to integrate various types of learning, develop thinking skills, and encourage self-assessment and independent learning, the performance objectives should be stated and used in such a way that these intended outcomes are achieved. The following guidelines provide a framework for developing, stating, and using performance objectives in problem-solving projects.

1. *State the performance objectives at the proper level of instruction.* The performance outcomes need to be stated in terms that are understood by the students. Thus at the elementary level of instruction the statements need to be in simpler terminology, briefer, and more specific. One way to choose the appropriate terminology is to have students participate in developing the statements. Another is to present your list to students, explain the meaning of the statements, and then modify the statements in terms of the student's comments. Writing or rewriting the performance outcomes in terms familiar to students will make them more useful for self-directed learning and self-assessment by students.

2. *Adapt the statements to the area of instruction by using relevant terminology and types of outcomes.* Although performance objectives for problem solving are to encourage the integration of knowledge and skills from many different areas, the statements are more readily understood and viewed as fair if seen as outcomes relevant to the content area being studied.

3. *Use the specific performance outcomes as criteria for judging performance.* If the outcomes are well stated they can be used directly as criteria or put in question form.

For example, a specific outcome concerning a statement of the problem can be restated as follows:

States the problem clearly and objectively.

Is the problem stated clearly and objectively?

Stating the outcomes in question form is usually helpful to students in assessing their own work. In any event, when stating the performance outcomes, you should ask yourself: Is this specific outcome stated well enough to serve as a criterion for guiding learning and assessing the performance?

4. *Develop and make the list of performance outcomes available to students before beginning work on the problem-solving projects.* The list of performance outcomes (i.e., criteria) should be used both in guiding learning and assessing the performance. They should be available to students early so they can be used in directing their own learning, in assessing their own progress, in improving their self-assessment skills, and in achieving independent learning—all goals of the problem-solving projects. A common practice is to have students compare their assessments with those of the teachers and to discuss any discrepancies in judgment. This provides an opportunity to improve both the students' learning and their self-assessment skills. It might also result in modifying some of the criteria to make them more relevant to the projects or more understandable to the students.

5. *Base the instruments to be used to assess learning on the specific performance outcomes.* Procedures for assessing the problem-solving project typically rely on judgments guided by checklists, rating scales, or some type of holistic scoring rubric (i.e., scoring guidelines) describing different levels of performance. The rating or scoring procedure should be based on the criteria derived from the lists of specific performance outcomes.

The procedures for assessing performance outcomes will be discussed and illustrated in Chapter 12. Here we will simply say that, as a rule, intended performance outcomes and assessment procedures must always be in close harmony, and the assessment procedures should be shared with students at the beginning of the instruction.

Summary

1. Problem-solving projects are useful for integrating learning and skills from many different areas, developing higher-level thinking skills, and providing opportunities for student self-assessment and independent learning.

2. Restricted problem-solving projects are limited in scope, highly structured, and typically assigned by the teacher.

3. Extended problem-solving projects are broad in scope, concerned with poorly structured problems that have many possible solutions (like those in the "real world"), and the students typically are free to select and study a problem of their choice.

4. Extended problem-solving projects may require the statement of performance outcomes for some or all of the following areas:

    a. Identifying and selecting a problem.

    b. Locating and selecting relevant resources.

    c. Writing a report describing the project.

    d. Conducting an experiment.

    e. Preparing display materials.

    f. Orally presenting and defending the project.

    g. Effectiveness in *group* problem solving.

5. The illustrative objectives and performance outcomes presented in this chapter are broad in scope to fit many types of problems, and are best used as models for stating performance outcomes that are more specific and relevant to a particular instructional area.

6. When writing specific performance outcomes for your instructional area and level of instruction, state them in terms that are clearly understood by students, that reflect the types of problems common to the content area, and that provide clear criteria for judging the performance.

7. Base the procedures used in assessing the problem-solving project directly on the criteria derived from the performance outcomes, and share the intended outcomes and assessment procedures with the students at the beginning of the project. This provides students with a focus for their learning and a basis for assessing their own learning progress.

Exercises

1. Using one of the generic examples of objectives for restricted problem-solving projects on page 94 as a model, write an objective for a restricted problem-solving project in an instructional area of interest to you.

2. Using one of the generic examples of objectives for extended problem-solving projects on pages 95 to 96 as a model, write an objective for an extended problem-solving project in an instructional area of interest to you.

3. Critique your objectives from Exercises 1 and 2 with these questions.

    a. Is the objective written in such a way that students would understand it?

    b. Does the objective reflect a common and worthwhile problem in the instructional area?

    c. Does the objective provide clear criteria for judging the performance?

Part III

Using Instructional Objectives in Assessment

Chapter 11

Using Objectives in Achievement Testing

INSTRUCTIONAL OBJECTIVE:

Uses objectives in achievement testing.

1. Describes how instructional objectives are used in achievement testing.
2. Explains the advantages of using a table of specifications in preparing tests.
3. Summarizes the procedure for preparing a table of specifications.
4. Describes how to prepare test items that are relevant to instructional objectives.
5. Describes the procedure for using detailed specifications for item writing.

Instructional objectives are key to your assessment of student achievement. They describe the types of performance students should be able to demonstrate at the end of instruction. Some types of student performance can be assessed by means of paper-and-pencil tests; others require the use of observation and judgment guided by rating scales, checklists, holistic scoring rubrics, or self-report methods. In this chapter, we will describe the use of objectives in achievement testing. In Chapter 12, we will describe their use in assessing performance skills and affective outcomes.

An achievement test is a device for measuring a sample of student performance. You can only have so many test items or questions, so the questions you do ask must be a good sample of all the possible questions you could ask. To provide a valid measure, the sample must be relevant and representative of what has been taught during the instruction. A satisfactory sample is most likely to be obtained if a systematic procedure is followed during test preparation. The following steps provide a useful procedure for this purpose:

1. State the general instructional objectives to be tested and define them in measurable terms.
2. Make an outline of the course content.

3. Prepare a table of specifications that describes the nature of the test sample.

4. Construct test items relevant to the table of specifications.

Each of these steps will be described and illustrated for a unit in economics.

Preparing the List of Instructional Objectives

When the instructional objectives have been defined by a list of specific learning outcomes stated in performance terms, they clarify the nature of the performance to be called forth by test items. The following list of instructional objectives illustrates how the objectives might be stated for a brief unit. The list is not exhaustive, but it clarifies the procedure for stating objectives for testing purposes.

Objectives for a Unit in Economics

1. Knows basic terms.
    1.1. Relates terms that have the same meaning.
    1.2. Selects the term that best fits a particular definition.
    1.3. Identifies terms used in reference to particular economic problems.
    1.4. Uses terms correctly in describing economic problems.

2. Comprehends economic concepts and principles.
    2.1. Identifies examples of economic concepts and principles.
    2.2. Describes economic concepts and principles in his or her own words.
    2.3. Identifies the interrelationship of economic principles.
    2.4. Explains changes in economic conditions in terms of the economic concepts and principles involved.

3. Applies economic principles to new situations.
    3.1. Identifies the economic principles needed to solve a practical problem.
    3.2. Predicts the probable outcome of an action involving economic principles.
    3.3. Describes how to solve a practical economic problem in terms of the economic principles involved.
    3.4. Distinguishes between probable and improbable economic forecasts.

4. Interprets economic data.
    4.1. Differentiates between relevant and irrelevant information.
    4.2. Differentiates between facts and inferences.
    4.3. Identifies cause–effect relations in data.
    4.4. Describes the trends in data.
    4.5. Distinguishes between warranted and unwarranted conclusions drawn from data.
    4.6. States proper qualifications when describing data.

Note that the statements of specific learning outcomes listed under each general objective describe how the students are expected to react toward the subject matter in economics but do not describe the specific subject matter toward which they are to react. Therefore, the specific statements listed under "Knows basic terms" describe what is meant by "knowing"—not what terms the students should know. Such statements make it possible to relate the objectives and the specific learning outcomes to various areas of content and thus to various units within the same course. As we shall see shortly, the table of specifications provides a method for relating the instructional objectives to the course content.

Outlining the Content

Because an achievement test should also adequately sample the content included in the instruction, an outline of the content is needed for the test. The same content outline that is used for teaching may suffice, or a less elaborate outline may be developed as part of the test plan. The following list of topics for our illustrative unit in economics provides sufficient detail for testing purposes.

Content Outline for a Unit in Economics (Money and Banking)

A. Forms and functions of money
   1. Types of money
   2. Various uses of money

B. Operation of banks
   1. Services provided by commercial banks
   2. Other institutions offering banking services
   3. Role of banks in managing the flow of money

C. Role of the Federal Reserve System
   1. Need for flexibility in the money supply
   2. Nature of the Federal Reserve System
   3. Regulatory policies influencing the money supply

D. State regulation of banks
   1. The state banking commission
   2. Laws to protect the borrowers

The amount of detail to be included in the outline of content will depend on the length of time covered by the instruction. For a two-week unit of work, you may be able to include all the major and minor topics. In outlining the content for an entire course, however, you may have to limit the outline to the main subject headings. Restricting the length of the outline to one or two pages is usually satisfactory for test-construction purposes.

Preparing the Table of Specifications

A table of specifications is a two-dimensional table that relates the instructional objectives to the course content. The table makes it possible to classify each test item in terms of both objectives and content. A completed table describes the number of test items needed to obtain a balanced measure of the instructional objectives and the course content emphasized in the instruction.

A sample table of specifications, based on our illustrative unit in economics, is shown in Table 11.1. To simplify the table, we have included only the general instructional objectives and major areas of content. This procedure is typical, although more detail may be desirable in some situations.

The numbers listed within the table indicate the number of test items to be constructed in each area. For example, a total of 15 items will measure the objective "Knows basic terms," including 3 items in the content area "Forms and functions of money," 4 in the content area "Operation of banks," and so on down the column. The total number of items in each column indicates the relative emphasis to be given to each objective, and the total number of items in each row indicates the relative emphasis to be given to each area of content. Therefore, the two-way grid specifies the test sample in terms of both instructional objectives and course content.

The relative emphasis shown in the table of specifications should reflect the emphasis given during instruction. This is accomplished by assigning weights to each objective and to each content area during the construction of the table. The usual procedure is first to distribute the total number (or percentage) of test items over the objectives and content areas and then to distribute the items among the individual points. Although a number of factors might be considered in assigning such weights, the amount of instructional time

Table 11.1   Table of Specifications for a 50-Item Test in Economics (Money and Banking)

	Instructional Objectives				
	1	**2**	**3**	**4**	
Content Areas	**Knows Basic Terms**	**Comprehends Concepts and Principles**	**Applies Principles**	**Interprets Data**	**Total Number of Test Items**
A. Forms and functions of money	3	4	3		10
B. Operation of banks	4	3	5	3	15
C. Role of the Federal Reserve System	4	6	3	2	15
D. State regulation of banks	4	2	4		10
Total number of test items	15	15	15	5	50

devoted to each area will usually provide a satisfactory approximation. Table 11.1, for instance, assumes that *Interprets data* (5 test items) received only one-third of the instructional emphasis given to each of the other objectives (15 test items each) and that this instruction was limited to content areas B and C. The table also indicates, by the number of items in each row, that content areas A and D received less instructional emphasis than areas B and C.

Constructing Relevant Test Items

The table of specifications describes the nature of the desired test sample and specifies what each test item should measure. The next task is to construct test items that are relevant to the instructional objectives and content areas of each cell. For example, let's use Table 11.1 to construct one of the four test items to measure the first objective ("Knows basic terms") in content area B ("Operation of banks"). Our procedure would be as follows: (1) to select one of the specific learning outcomes listed under the first objective, (2) to select one of the important banking terms, and (3) to construct a test item that calls forth the specific performance indicated in the learning outcome. Our test item should clearly reflect the desired learning outcome as follows:

Instructional Objective: 1. Knows basic terms.

Learning Outcome: 1.1. Relates terms that have the same meaning.

  1. Checking accounts are also called:

    A. Credit money

    B. Currency

   *C. Demand deposits

    D. Time deposits

  Note in the above example that the learning outcome describes the specific response we expect the students to demonstrate and that the test item presents a relevant task. Other examples at the comprehension and application levels are presented below. The objectives and outcomes are from our illustrative list of objectives for a unit in economics and are numbered accordingly.

Instructional Objective: 2. Comprehends economic concepts and principles.

Learning Outcome: 2.1. Identifies examples of economic concepts.

  1. Which one of the following is an example of commercial credit?

   *A. A manufacturer borrows money to buy raw materials.

    B. A manufacturer borrows money to build a new plant.

    C. A business executive borrows money to build a new house.

    D. A stockbroker borrows money to buy stocks and bonds.

*indicates correct answer

Table 11.2   Simple Table for Item Writing (Elementary Math)

Specific Learning Outcomes	Test Items
Computation of fractions	4
Computation of decimals	4
Computation of percents	4
Conversions between fractions and decimals	4
Conversions between fractions and percents	4
Conversions between decimals and percents	4
Application to life problems (e.g., sales, loans, etc.)	6
Total test items	30

Instructional Objective: 3. Applies economic principles to new situations.

Learning Outcome: 3.2. Predicts the possible outcome of an action involving economic principles.

1. Which one of the following actions of the Federal Reserve Board would most likely contribute to greater inflation?

   A. Buying government bonds on the open market

   B. Raising the reserve requirements

   C. Raising the discount rate

   D. Lowering the amount of credit granted to member banks

Using a Simple Table for Item Writing

It is not always necessary to use a two-dimensional table of specifications for item writing. When planning a brief review test or preparing a test to locate common learning errors, a one-way classification, like the one in Table 11.2, may suffice. It merely lists the specific learning outcomes and the number of test items for each. Such a table provides greater assurance that a sample of all-important elements is covered and it helps pinpoint areas where students are having difficulty.

Using Detailed Specifications for Item Writing

When teachers prepare test items cooperatively, as for a departmental examination or for storage in item banks, detailed specifications may be useful for item writing. In this case, the general instructional objective and the specific learning outcomes to be tested are stated, the type of test item to be used is indicated, and characteristics of the item are briefly described and illustrated with a sample test item. Examples of such specifications in two skill areas are presented in Boxes 11.1 and 11.2.

Box 11.1   Writing

General instructional objective: Knows fundamentals of written expression.

Specific learning outcome: Distinguishes between complete and incomplete sentences.

Type of test items: Multiple choice (10 items)

Item characteristics: Each test item will contain one complete sentence and three incomplete sentences. The *stem* of the item will tell the student to choose the complete sentence. The *correct response* will be a complete sentence. The *incorrect alternatives* (distracters) will be sentence fragments.

Sample item:

Choose the *complete* sentence.

  A. The children who went to the zoo.
  B. The monkeys in the zoo swinging.
  C. Going to the zoo was fun.
  D. Whatever you think of the zoo.

Box 11.2   Math

General instructional objective: Comprehends our number system.

Specific learning outcome: Identifies place value.

Type of test items: Multiple choice (10 items)

Item characteristics: Each test item will contain a stem in the form of a question or incomplete statement, followed by four alternative answers. The *stem* of the item will contain a whole number with three to six digits. The student will be asked to identify the value of two of the digits by indicating the degree to which one is a multiple of the other. The *correct response* will indicate an understanding of the place value of both digits. The *incorrect alternatives* (distracters) will consist of common errors in identifying place value.

Sample item:

In the number 9,632, the 9 has a value that is

  A. Three times the value of the 3
  B. Thirty times the value of the 3
  C. Three hundred times the value of the 3
  D. Three thousand times the value of the 3

Using detailed specifications makes it more likely that you will be able to prepare a functionally equivalent set of relevant test items for each specific learning outcome, even if several teachers are constructing the items. The detail is also useful in clarifying the meaning of the results during test interpretation.

When you use detailed specifications, the table of specifications, discussed earlier, still plays an important role. It provides an overall framework for preparing an item bank and it provides a guide for selecting items from the bank when preparing a test for a particular use. More detailed information on test specifications and item writing can be found in Brookhart and Nitko (2008), Gronlund (2006), and Nitko and Brookhart (2007).

Using Objectives for Interpreting Test Results

The instructional objectives used to construct a test can also be used to interpret the results. For example, you can use the list of specific learning outcomes in Table 11.2 to report back to students how well they did on the test. A report by specific learning outcomes will indicate each student's strengths and weaknesses and identify areas where remedial work would be most beneficial. Remedial lessons and practice problems could be made available for each outcome, so that the students could work on their weaknesses independently.

In addition to using the specific learning outcomes for immediate feedback to students, instructional objectives are also useful for a more general report on progress. You can use a report such as the one in Figure 11.1 to indicate how well students are achieving the general objectives of a unit or course. This form may be used as a periodic progress report or incorporated into the school's grading system. A description of how well the objectives are being achieved by students is a good supplement to the commonly used letter grade. When used with a letter grade, it is of course important that all of the relevant objectives be listed.

Figure 11.1   Achievement Report Based on Table 11.1 (Economics)

Directions: Circle the number that indicates the student's level of achievement on each of the general objectives listed below.

4 - High achievement on intended outcomes

3 - Satisfactory achievement, some weaknesses

2 - Low achievement, additional work needed

1 - Objective not achieved

4 3 2 1   (a) Knows basic terms.
4 3 2 1   (b) Comprehends economic concepts and principles.
4 3 2 1   (c) Applies economic principles to new situations.
4 3 2 1   (d) Interprets economic data.

Summary

1. Instructional objectives play a key role in the testing of student achievement by describing the types of performance to be measured.

2. A table of specifications is a useful guide for constructing a test that measures a relevant and representative sample of student performance.

3. A table of specifications is a two-dimensional table that indicates the nature and number of test items needed to obtain a balanced measure of the intended learning outcomes.

4. Relevant test items are obtained by constructing items that call forth the student performance described in the specific learning outcome.

5. A one-way classification table may be useful when planning for a brief classroom test. Such a table provides for the measurement of a balanced sample of learning outcomes and aids in pinpointing areas of learning difficulty.

6. Detailed specifications for writing test items may be useful where teachers are preparing items cooperatively for departmental examinations or storage in item banks.

7. Instructional objectives can be used to interpret assessment results to students. This may be done in terms of the specific learning outcomes or the general objectives, depending on the purpose of the report.

Exercises

1. Describe how you would use instructional objectives in achievement testing for a unit of instruction in a content area and grade level of interest to you.

2. How do you use instructional objectives and a content outline, respectively, to write (or select) test items?

Chapter 12

Using Objectives in Performance and Affective Assessment

INSTRUCTIONAL OBJECTIVE:

Uses objectives in performance and affective assessment.

1. Describes how instructional objectives are used in performance and affective assessment.
2. Distinguishes between analytic and holistic scoring.
3. Lists the steps in using instructional objectives to construct rating scales, checklists, and holistic scoring rubrics.
4. Lists the steps in preparing an attitude scale.
5. Describes how instructional objectives can contribute to the use of student portfolios.
6. Lists the guidelines for preparing and using assessment instruments.

A number of important learning outcomes cannot be measured by the traditional paper-and-pencil test. Most of these require the assessment of performance skills (e.g., communication skills, laboratory skills, vocational skills) or affective outcomes (e.g., attitudes, interests, values). Assessing these types of learning depends on judgments of the ongoing process, the product resulting from the process, or both. Typically some type of observational instrument (e.g., rating scale or checklist) or scoring guide (e.g., scoring rubric) is used to direct and record your judgments. The method depends to a large extent on the type of information you are seeking and, thus, the scoring procedure to be used.

Assessing Performance Skills

In performance assessment, the specific learning outcomes for each objective provide the criteria for judging the quality of the performance. In some cases you may want to make separate judgments on each criterion. This is called *analytical scoring* and uses a rating scale, checklist, or rubric for each criterion. The main advantage of this procedure is that it provides a diagnostic picture of a student's strengths and weaknesses, and thus provides a basis for improving performance. However, in some cases you may want to consider the criteria as a whole and make an overall assessment of performance. This requires the use of *holistic scoring*.

Holistic scoring classifies the overall performance into one of a number of categories based on level of quality. Each category may be then briefly described by degrees to which the overall criteria have been satisfied. These scoring guides are called *holistic scoring rubrics*. Holistic scoring is defended on the basis that the whole is more than the sum of its parts. In assessing a speech, for example, your impression may be that it was a good speech even though the speaker violated some of the common rules of speaking. Likewise, in assessing a product like writing, you may conclude that it is excellent writing even though the organization, vocabulary, and style do not follow the usual pattern. Thus, this overall impression of the performance or product provides something different from what you would get by simply summing the scores obtained from analytical scoring. Holistic scoring takes less time than analytic scoring and is useful when you need a summative judgment (as for a grade) but do not need the formative information analytic scoring would provide.

There is, of course, no reason why both holistic and analytic scoring cannot be used for the same performance or product. One provides the overall judgment and the other provides useful diagnostic information. However, where both are used, the overall judgment should be made first so that it is less likely to be distorted by a low rating on some specific element.

Rating Scales

The rating scale provides a convenient observational guide for analytical scoring. It (1) focuses attention on the specific elements of the performance to be observed, and (2) provides a convenient method of recording the judgments of the observer. Typically a rating scale can be prepared easily by using the specific learning outcomes as criteria for judging the performance and adding a scale for rating on each specific item.

Let's assume that the following performance objective and list of specific outcomes have been written for a science course (taken from Chapter 9):

1. Uses laboratory equipment properly.

    1.1. Selects appropriate equipment for an experiment.

    1.2. Assembles equipment correctly for the experiment.

    1.3. Manipulates equipment as needed during the experiment.

    1.4. Measures accurately with proper measuring device.

    1.5. Follows safety rules in conducting experiment.

    1.6. Uses materials without wasting any.

Figure 12.1   Sample Rating Scale Items

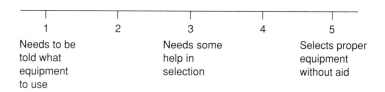

1.1 Selects appropriate equipment

1	2	3	4	5
Needs to be told what equipment to use		Needs some help in selection		Selects proper equipment without aid

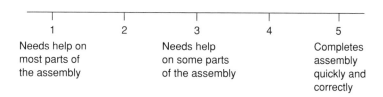

1.2 Assembles equipment correctly

1	2	3	4	5
Needs help on most parts of the assembly		Needs help on some parts of the assembly		Completes assembly quickly and correctly

   1.7. Completes experiment on time.

   1.8. Cleans equipment and returns to proper place.

Each of these specific outcomes can serve as items in a *rating scale* by simply modifying the wording slightly and by adding a place beneath each item to record the ratings, as shown in Figure 12.1.

The complete rating scale would include (1) items covering all specific outcomes to be judged, (2) directions for making the ratings, and (3) possibly a place for comments beneath each rating scale item. All we are doing here is illustrating how easy it is to construct a rating scale when the intended outcomes have been clearly specified. The specific outcomes indicate the performance to be observed and become the items in the rating instrument. The graphic scale beneath each item simply provides a place to record the ratings. A more compact type of rating scale can be made by listing a set of numbers in front of each specific outcome and describing the meaning of the numbers in the directions. A scale of this type for the procedures and product of a woodworking project (taken from Chapter 9) is shown in Figure 12.2.

This numerical rating scale, like the graphic scale, again simply uses the stated specific outcomes as the items in the scale. If the outcomes are carefully stated, making a rating scale is a simple task. Also, stating them in terms students can understand makes it possible for students to rate their own performance or product and compare it with the teacher's rating. A conference discussing the discrepancies in ratings can contribute to both improved student performance and improved student self-assessment skills.

Checklists

In assessing some types of performance, the judgment on each performance criterion requires a simple yes-or-no response. For example, in observing a procedure we may be

Figure 12.2   Sample Numerical Rating Scale

Directions: Rate each of the following items by circling the appropriate number:
4 = Advanced,   3 = Proficient,   2 = Basic,   1 = Below Basic

Follows proper procedures
4 3 2 1 (a) Follows the steps listed in the project plan.
4 3 2 1 (b) Selects appropriate materials to use.
4 3 2 1 (c) Selects proper tools for project.
4 3 2 1 (d) Uses tools correctly for each task.
4 3 2 1 (e) Works carefully to avoid waste of material.
4 3 2 1 (f) Uses time efficiently and completes project on schedule.

Constructs a satisfactory product
4 3 2 1 (a) Dimensions of product match specifications.
4 3 2 1 (b) Overall appearance reflects care in construction.
4 3 2 1 (c) Finish is even and of high quality.
4 3 2 1 (d) Joints are smooth and fit tightly.
4 3 2 1 (e) Parts (e.g., drawers) fit properly and function well.

interested only in determining whether a specific action was taken. In judging a product, we may be concerned only about the presence or absence of each specific characteristic. In these cases, the list of performance steps or product characteristics can be assessed by means of a *checklist*.

The checklist, like the rating scale, (1) is derived directly from the list of specific outcomes that describes the procedure or product, (2) directs attention to the significant elements to be observed, and (3) provides a convenient method of recording the observations. The main difference between them is in the type of judgment to be made. The rating scale calls for a judgment concerning the degree to which a characteristic is present, whereas the checklist calls for a judgment of present or absent. An illustrative checklist, based on a performance objective in Chapter 9, is shown in Figure 12.3.

Checklists are also useful with those products that require a simple judgment concerning whether a characteristic is present or absent. The list of outcomes for constructing a bar graph (from Chapter 9), for example, does not imply that the degree of each characteristic is important. Therefore, a checklist will suffice, as illustrated in Figure 12.4. Of course, in cases where the degree to which each characteristic is present provides a more adequate assessment of a product, the rating scale should be used.

As with the rating scale, the items listed in a checklist should be stated in terms that are readily understood by students, so they can use the list to check their own performance and develop self-assessment skills.

Figure 12.3   Checklist for Evaluating the Proper Application of Varnish

Directions: On the space in front of each item, place a plus (+) sign if performance is satisfactory, place a minus (–) sign if it is unsatisfactory.

_____ 1. Sands and prepares surface properly.
_____ 2. Wipes dust from surface with appropriate cloth.
_____ 3. Selects appropriate brush.
_____ 4. Selects varnish and checks varnish flow.
_____ 5. Pours needed amount of varnish into clean container.
_____ 6. Puts brush properly into varnish (1/3 of bristle length).
_____ 7. Wipes excess varnish from brush on inside edge of container.
_____ 8. Applies varnish to surface with smooth strokes.
_____ 9. Works from center of surface toward the edges.
_____ 10. Brushes with the grain of the wood.
_____ 11. Uses light strokes to smooth the varnish.
_____ 12. Checks surface for completeness.
_____ 13. Cleans brush with appropriate cleaner.
_____ 14. Does not pour excess varnish back into can.
_____ 15. Cleans work area.

Figure 12.4   Checklist for Evaluating the Construction of a Bar Graph

Directions: On the space in front of each item, place a plus (+) sign if the characteristic is present, place a minus (–) sign if characteristic is absent.

_____ 1. Uses a separate bar for each measure.
_____ 2. Matches length of each bar to data.
_____ 3. Arranges bars in some logical order.
_____ 4. Makes bars wider than space between them.
_____ 5. Uses scale and guidelines that make bars easy to interpret.
_____ 6. Identifies each bar with a label.
_____ 7. Uses title that clearly indicates nature of the graph.

Holistic Scoring Rubrics

As noted earlier, holistic scoring is based on a person's impression of the performance skill or product. When these types of judgments are made, the judges typically place the performance or product into one of several categories. A commonly used number of categories is 4 or 6. An even number is used so that a middle category doesn't become a dumping ground. The judgment and placement in a category is usually aided by a *holistic scoring rubric*. These scoring rubrics describe the qualities at each level of performance and are derived from the intended performance outcomes. Using scoring rubrics makes it possible to express the level of proficiency by either a descriptive label or a number (e.g., Advanced—4, Proficient—3, Basic—2, and Below Basic—1).

A sample scoring rubric for assessing a written report of a problem-solving project is presented in Figure 12.5. The descriptions for each level are from the list of performance outcomes in Chapter 10. They are more fully stated here than they might be for a scoring rubric to illustrate their derivation from the stated performance outcomes. In some cases, it may be desirable to modify or abbreviate them for scoring purposes. Just make sure that the key elements are included in the list of criteria.

Figure 12.5 Scoring Rubric for the Written Report of a Problem-Solving Project

4. Description of problem and study procedures is outstanding.

   Thorough analysis, synthesis, and interpretation of findings.

   Clearly stated conclusions that are supported by the findings.

   Comprehensive description of limitations of the study and the need for further research.

3. Description of problem and study procedures is good.

   Fairly thorough analysis, synthesis, and interpretation of findings.

   Conclusions are clear and generally supported by findings.

   Descriptions of limitations of study and the need for further research could be more detailed.

2. Description of problem and study procedures is weak.

   Limited analysis, synthesis, and interpretation of findings.

   Conclusions are rather general and not fully supported by findings.

   Descriptions of limitations of study and the need for further research are brief and general.

1. Description of problem and study procedures is unclear.

   Attempts at analysis, synthesis, and interpretation are incomplete.

   Conclusions are general and not in harmony with findings.

   Description of limitations of study and the need for further research are missing or inadequate.

In some cases, it may be desirable to combine holistic scoring with analytical scoring. For example, a rating scale or rubrics may be developed for analytical scoring with a place provided at the beginning for the overall judgment of the performance or product. This makes it possible to record the general impression first and then to clarify the overall judgment by noting strengths and weaknesses on the rating scale items.

Assessing Affective Outcomes

The assessment of affective outcomes is much more difficult than the assessment of cognitive outcomes or performance skills. Students' feelings and emotions are more controlled and may be concealed by expected social behavior. Thus, in addition to routine classroom observation, you need to use a variety of assessment techniques to supplement our observations and judgments. Here again, checklists and rating scales are useful, as are self-report methods that attempt to assess students' internal states (e.g., attitudes and interests).

Rating Scales and Checklists

As with performance assessment, the instruments used to assess affective outcomes are fashioned from the lists of intended learning outcomes. Thus, rating scale construction begins with a list of the specific learning outcomes, then a scale for rating, and then a set of directions are added. For example, the rating scale illustrated in Figure 12.6 is based on the list of affective outcomes presented in Chapter 8. These items were put in rating scale form because frequency of occurrence was the focus. A simple rating scale like this one is sometimes used at the lower elementary level and a more detailed rating scale is used at higher levels of instruction. In either case, however, the items are derived directly from the list of affective outcomes.

When you prepare rating scales in the affective area, it is important to limit the statements to observable behavior. In Figure 12.6, for example, we have listed overt behavior that reflects attitude toward learning math and not statements concerning how students feel

Figure 12.6   Rating Scale for Attitude Toward Learning (Elementary Math)

Directions: Rate each of the following items by circling the appropriate number.

    3 = Always

    2 = Sometimes

    1 = Never

3 2 1 (a) Pays attention when problems are explained.
3 2 1 (b) Follows directions when solving problems.
3 2 1 (c) Works independently when solving problems.
3 2 1 (d) Asks questions when a procedure is not clear.
3 2 1 (e) Completes class assignments on time.

Figure 12.7 Checklist for Evaluating Safe Use of Laboratory Equipment

Directions: Circle YES or NO to indicate your response.

YES NO   1. Examines equipment before using.
YES NO   2. Wears appropriate safety gear.
YES NO   3. Uses care in setting up equipment.
YES NO   4. Follows safe procedures in using equipment.
YES NO   5. Dismantles equipment carefully.
YES NO   6. Cleans and restores equipment when done.

about math. Later we will describe a self-report instrument that can be used to determine a student's attitude toward a subject by expressing how he or she feels, but rating scales must focus on observable behavior.

As with performance assessment, some affective outcomes can be assessed with a simple checklist like the one in Figure 12.7. The use of a checklist, like this one, is appropriate if the form is to be used after a particular laboratory session. If the judgments are to be made in a summative assessment over numerous laboratory sessions, then a rating scale indicating frequency of occurrence would be more appropriate. Both types of instruments are simply procedures for directing one's observations and recording the judgments made.

Self-Report Method

Some affective outcomes require the use of a self-report method such as the *attitude scale.* For example, attitude toward school, toward a particular course, toward laboratory work, or some activity may be considered an important learning outcome. Although some information can be obtained by observation, obtaining self-report data concerning attitudes can provide a meaningful supplement to observation.

As with other assessment techniques, the attitude scale should be prepared in harmony with outcomes to be evaluated. For example, describing in specific terms what is meant by a "favorable attitude toward science" provides the basis for selecting statements that are clearly favorable and clearly unfavorable for use in an attitude scale like the one shown in Figure 12.8. This Likert-type scale uses five alternatives and favorable items, like the first one, are scored by using values of 5, 4, 3, 2, 1, going from SA (strongly agree) to SD (strongly disagree). To score unfavorable items, like the second one, reverse the values to 1, 2, 3, 4, 5, going from SA to SD. An individual's score on this type of scale is the sum of the scores on all items, with a higher score indicating a more favorable attitude. If an intended learning outcome in the area of attitudes has been carefully defined, a Likert-type scale can be easily prepared, scored, and interpreted.

One way to obtain favorable and unfavorable statements for a Likert-type scale is to ask students to list such statements. For example, in building a scale for attitude toward laboratory work, ask students to list all the favorable comments students might make about laboratory work and all the unfavorable comments. You can sift through these for ideas on the type of comments that are most frequent. This also helps you phrase the statements in

Figure 12.8   Illustrative Likert-Type Attitude Scale for Measuring Attitude Toward a Science Course

---

Directions: Indicate how much you agree or disagree with each statement by circling the appropriate letter(s).

	SA — Strongly Agree
	A — Agree
KEY	U — Undecided
	D — Disagree
	SD — Strongly Disagree

SA   A   U   D   SD   1. Science classes are interesting.

SA   A   U   D   SD   2. Science laboratory is dull and boring.

SA   A   U   D   SD   3. It is fun working on science problems.

SA   A   U   D   SD   4. Class activities are good.

SA   A   U   D   SD   5. Reading the textbook is a waste of time.

SA   A   U   D   SD   6. The laboratory experiments are interesting.

SA   A   U   D   SD   7. Most class activities are monotonous.

SA   A   U   D   SD   8. I enjoy reading the textbook.

SA   A   U   D   SD   9. The problems we are studying are unimportant.

SA   A   U   D   SD   10. I am *not* very enthusiastic about science.

---

language that is commonly used by students. Adapting student input to the statements of intended learning outcomes should result in a good collection of positive and negative statements that can be fashioned into a Likert-type scale.

When you use self-report methods such as an attitude scale, it is important to obtain students' responses anonymously. Students are unlikely to give honest responses if they can be identified. This poses no great problem in assessing students' attitudes, however. We should be mainly interested in how the instruction is changing attitudes, and not which students are changing most. For example, if students' attitude scores become more favorable toward science during the instruction, then we are meeting our objective.

The purpose of assessing attitudes is to monitor students' progress on valued learning objectives. Some of these are affective in nature. For example, teaching a student to read is only the beginning. A disposition to read and an interest in reading are important, too. Use attitude assessment to inform your teaching. Do not use attitude assessments as part of a grade. If students discover a "good" attitude report will get them a good grade, they will not be able to be honest in their reporting.

Using Student Portfolios

In some schools, students keep portfolios containing samples of their school performances. This might include samples of writing, drawing, math problems, research reports, test results, ratings, and checklists of performance skills and affective outcomes. The samples are typically collected and sequenced so that learning progress can be judged (e.g., improvement in writing skills, drawing skills, or problem-solving ability). The portfolio is an especially useful method for communicating to both students and parents the degree of student improvement. Nothing makes clearer the actual changes in student performance than a comparison of sample work obtained at different times during the instruction.

In some instances, a portfolio may be limited to one type of skill (e.g., writing). In others, a portfolio of all classroom work might be assembled for a more complete assessment of learning progress. Regardless of the nature and scope of the portfolio, there are four basic questions to consider in using this technique: (1) What is the purpose—what is the portfolio evidence intended to show? (2) What types of evidence should be included in the portfolio? (3) Should the portfolio samples be based on assigned exercises or should routine classwork be collected? (4) How are the portfolio samples to be assessed—including whether and how to include student reflections? A set of instructional objectives defined in terms of intended learning outcomes can serve as a guide for all four decisions.

The list of instructional objectives makes clear what performance tasks are needed to fill in gaps and supplement paper-and-pencil testing. For example, a test of knowledge outcomes (e.g., elements of grammar) will need to be supplemented by an assessment of application outcomes (e.g., writing samples). In addition, the specific learning outcomes that define each objective can help decide whether a performance exercise needs to be assigned (e.g., write a short story) or typical samples of classwork should be collected (e.g., daily written work). Finally, the list of objectives and specific learning outcomes can aid in both teacher assessment and student reflection on the portfolio samples by specifying the precise nature of the student performance to be judged.

The portfolio is especially useful for evaluating complex performance outcomes (e.g., thinking skills) and affective outcomes (e.g., attitudes) because changes are frequently subtle and take place over long periods of time. Thus, the periodic collection of recorded observations, rating scales, and checklists can make the subtle changes over time more apparent and thus more useful in judging student progress. A more complete description of how student portfolios are used in assessing student progress can be found in Gronlund (2006) and in Nitko and Brookhart (2007).

Guidelines for Preparing and Using Assessment Instruments

Throughout this chapter our main goal has been to describe and illustrate how well-defined instructional objectives can be used in assessing performance skills and affective outcomes. When instructional objectives are defined in terms of intended learning outcomes, they clarify precisely what is to be assessed, they provide a guide for selecting and preparing assessment instruments, and they aid in the interpretation of results. If a portfolio is used, objectives can also aid in determining the type of evidence that is to be included and the criteria to be used in assessing the portfolio samples.

The following suggestions provide guidelines to keep in mind when preparing assessment instruments from instructional objectives and using them to improve learning.

1. Check to be sure that the specific learning outcomes include the most important elements of each objective.
2. Use the intended learning outcomes as criteria for preparing the assessment instrument.
3. Select the type of assessment instrument that best evaluates the performance skills or affective outcomes.
4. Prepare an instrument that is understandable and easy to use by students.
5. Use an appropriate scoring procedure (i.e., holistic for overall judgment, analytic for judgment on each criterion).
6. Share the assessment instruments with students before instruction begins and have students use them to assess their own learning progress during instruction.
7. If students are mature enough, have them participate in preparing the assessment instruments.
8. If a portfolio of schoolwork is to be kept by each student, use the instructional objectives and specific learning outcomes as a framework for selecting and assessing the portfolio samples to be included.

Throughout this chapter and Chapter 11 the focus has been on how to use objectives and specific learning outcomes in the assessment of learning. No attempt was made to discuss student assessment in any great detail. For more elaborate descriptions and illustrations of how to assess learning outcomes, and for reference to many other books about student assessment, see Brookhart and Nitko (2008), Gronlund (2006), and Nitko and Brookhart (2007). It is simply our contention here that basing assessment on clearly stated intended learning outcomes results in more comprehensive and valid evidence of student learning.

Summary

1. Instructional objectives play a key role in assessing performance skills and affective outcomes by describing the relevant aspects to be judged (i.e., they provide the criteria for assessment).
2. Performance skills may be assessed during analytical scoring (i.e., a separate judgment on each criterion) or holistic scoring (i.e., a general impression of the performance or product).
3. Analytical scoring is typically done by using a rating scale for recording the degree to which an element is present, or by using a checklist that simply requires a judgment of present or absent.
4. A rating scale or checklist can be prepared by listing the specific learning outcomes as items to be judged and adding a scale for responding to each item.
5. Holistic scoring typically uses a scoring guide, called a holistic scoring rubric, that classifies the performance or product into one of several categories (e.g., Advanced,

Proficient, Basic, Below Basic). An even number is used to avoid a middle dumping ground, and four or six categories are commonly used.

6. Affective outcomes that are observable can be judged with the aid of a rating scale or a checklist. As with performance skills, the items in the observation instrument are derived from the list of specific learning outcomes.

7. Affective outcomes based on inner feelings, such as attitudes, typically are assessed with self-report methods. The attitude scale is probably the most commonly used one in teaching. Its use requires anonymous responses if the results are to be valid.

8. A portfolio of samples of student performance is useful for assessing learning progress and for communicating the amount of improvement to students and parents. Stating the objectives in performance terms provides a framework for determining what portfolio samples to include (e.g., writing, drawing, problem solving) and provides the basis for their assessment.

9. A portfolio is especially useful in evaluating complex performance skills and affective behavior because the changes are subtle and take a long time to develop. The periodic collection of evidence makes the changes more apparent and thus more useful in judging student performance.

10. The preparation and use of assessment instruments are more likely to be effective where the objectives and specific learning outcomes have been clearly stated, the appropriate assessment and scoring methods have been selected, the assessment instruments are understandable and easy to use by students, the assessment instruments are shared with students before instruction begins, and are used by students during instruction to assess their own learning progress.

11. When assessment instruments are based on well-stated intended learning outcomes, they provide more comprehensive and valid evidence of student learning.

Exercises

1. Select one of the instructional objectives in Chapter 9 for a skill (pages 86–87) or product (page 88) and use them to do the following exercises.

   a. Construct a checklist to evaluate students' skill or product outcomes.

   b. Construct a rating scale or rubric to evaluate students' skill or product outcomes.

   c. Identify whether your scales in (a) and (b) are analytic or holistic and tell why.

2. Select one of the instructional objectives in Chapter 8 for affective outcomes (pages 78–79 or 79–80) and use them to do the following exercises.

   a. Construct a checklist to evaluate students' affective outcomes.

   b. Construct a rating scale to evaluate students' affective outcomes.

   c. Which (the checklist or the rating scale) do you think is more useful for the objective you selected? Explain why.

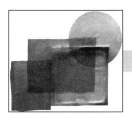

Appendix A

Checklist for Evaluating the Final List of Objectives

In this book we have described and illustrated how to identify and define instructional objectives in terms of student performance. Our focus was on the *stating* of the objectives and the specific learning outcomes. Questions such as "Which objectives are most desirable for a particular instructional unit?" we leave to the curriculum specialist and subject expert. In evaluating your final list of objectives, however, you might want to appraise the adequacy of the list, as well as how clearly the statements indicate your instructional intent. Therefore, general criteria for evaluating the final list of objectives and specific learning outcomes have been incorporated into this checklist.

The checklist is intended as a diagnostic tool for detecting and correcting errors in the final list of objectives. Any negative answer indicates an area where improvement is needed. The checklist is also useful, of course, as a guide for developing the original list of instructional objectives.

Checklist

Yes/No

Adequacy of the List of General Instructional Objectives

_____ 1. Does each general instructional objective indicate an appropriate outcome for the instructional unit? (See state standards, district curriculum, and recommendations of curriculum and subject experts.)

_____ 2. Does the list of general instructional objectives include all logical outcomes of the unit (knowledge, comprehension, application, skills, attitudes, and so on)?

_____ 3. Are the general instructional objectives attainable (do they take into account the students' background, facilities, time available, and so on)?

_____   4. Are the general instructional objectives in harmony with the philosophy of the school?

_____   5. Are the general instructional objectives in harmony with sound principles of learning (e.g., are the outcomes those that are most permanent and transferable)?

Statements of General Instructional Objectives

_____   6. Does each general instructional objective begin with a *verb* (e.g., knows, comprehends, appreciates)?

_____   7. Is each general instructional objective stated in terms of *student performance* (rather than teacher performance)?

_____   8. Is each general instructional objective stated as a learning product (rather than in terms of the learning process)?

_____   9. Is each general instructional objective stated in terms of the students' *terminal performance* (rather than the subject matter to be covered)?

_____   10. Does each general instructional objective include only one general learning outcome?

_____   11. Is each general instructional objective stated at the proper level of generality (i.e., is it clear, concise, and readily definable)?

_____   12. Is each general instructional objective stated so that it is relatively independent (i.e., free from overlap with other objectives)?

Statements of Specific Learning Outcomes

_____   13. Is each general instructional objective defined by a list of specific learning outcomes that describes the specific types of performance students are expected to demonstrate?

_____   14. Does each specific learning outcome begin with a *verb* that specifies definite, *observable performance* (e.g., identifies, describes, lists)?

_____   15. Is the performance described in each specific learning outcome relevant to the general instructional objective?

_____   16. Is there a sufficient number of specific learning outcomes to describe adequately the performance of students who have achieved each of the general instructional objectives?

_____   17. Is each specific learning outcome stated so that it can be used with various units of study?

_____   18. Is each specific learning outcome appropriate for the area and level of instruction?

Appendix B

Taxonomy of Educational Objectives (Major Categories and Illustrative Objectives)

Table B.1   Major Categories in the Cognitive Domain of the Taxonomy of Educational Objectives

Descriptions of the Major Categories in the Cognitive Domain

1. **Knowledge.** Knowledge is defined as the remembering of previously learned material. This may involve the recall of a wide range of material, from specific facts to complete theories, but all that is required is the bringing to mind of the appropriate information. Knowledge represents the lowest level of learning outcomes in the cognitive domain.

2. **Comprehension.** Comprehension is defined as the ability to grasp the meaning of material. This may be shown by translating material from one form to another (words to numbers), by interpreting material (explaining or summarizing), and by estimating future trends (predicting consequences or effects). These learning outcomes go one step beyond the simple remembering of material, and represent the lowest level of understanding.

3. **Application.** Application refers to the ability to use learned material in new and concrete situations. This may include the application of such things as rules, methods, concepts, principles, laws, and theories. Learning outcomes in this area require a higher level of understanding than those under comprehension.

4. **Analysis.** Analysis refers to the ability to break down material into its component parts so that its organizational structure may be understood. This may include the identification of the parts, analysis of the relationships between parts, and recognition of the organizational principles involved. Learning outcomes here represent a higher intellectual level than comprehension and application because they require an understanding of both the content and the structural form of the material.

5. **Synthesis.** Synthesis refers to the ability to put parts together to form a new whole. This may involve the production of a unique communication (theme or speech), a plan of operations (research proposal), or a set of abstract relations (scheme for classifying information). Learning outcomes in this area stress creative behaviors, with major emphasis on the formulation of *new* patterns of structures.

6. **Evaluation.** Evaluation is concerned with the ability to judge the value of material (statement, novel, poem, research report) for a given purpose. The judgments are to be based on definite criteria. These may be internal criteria (organization) or external criteria (relevance to the purpose), and the student may determine the criteria or be given them. Learning outcomes in this area are highest in the cognitive hierarchy because they contain elements of all of the other categories, plus conscious value judgments based on clearly defined criteria.

Note: Material in first column from Benjamin S. Bloom et al., *Taxonomy of Educational Objectives: Book 1, Cognitive Domain.* Published by Allyn and Bacon, Boston, MA. Copyright © 1984 by Pearson Education. Adapted by permission of the publisher.

Illustrative General Instructional Objectives	Illustrative Verbs for Stating Specific Learning Outcomes
Knows common terms Knows specific facts Knows methods and procedures Knows basic concepts Knows principles	Defines, describes, identifies, labels, lists, matches, names, outlines, reproduces, selects, states
Comprehends facts and principles Interprets verbal material Interprets charts and graphs Translates verbal material to mathematical formulas Estimates future consequences implied in data Justifies methods and procedures	Converts, defends, distinguishes, estimates, explains, extends, generalizes, gives examples, infers, paraphrases, predicts, rewrites, summarizes
Applies concepts and principles to new situations Applies laws and theories to practical situations Solves mathematical problems Constructs charts and graphs Demonstrates correct usage of a method or procedure	Changes, computes, demonstrates, discovers, manipulates, modifies, operates, predicts, prepares, produces, relates, shows, solves, uses
Recognizes unstated assumptions Recognizes logical fallacies in reasoning Distinguishes between facts and inferences Evaluates the relevancy of data Analyzes the organizational structure of a work (art, music, writing)	Breaks down, diagrams, differentiates, discriminates, distinguishes, identifies, illustrates, infers, outlines, points out, relates, selects, separates, subdivides
Writes a well-organized theme Gives a well-organized speech Writes a creative short story (or poem, or music) Proposes a plan for an experiment Integrates learning from different areas into a plan for solving a problem Formulates a new scheme for classifying objects (or events, or ideas)	Categorizes, combines, compiles, composes, creates, devises, designs, explains, generates, modifies, organizes, plans, rearranges, reconstructs, relates, reorganizes, revises, rewrites, summarizes, tells, writes
Judges the logical consistency of written material Judges the adequacy with which conclusions are supported by data Judges the value of a work (art, music, writing) by use of internal criteria Judges the value of a work (art, music, writing) by use of external standards of excellence	Appraises, compares, concludes, contrasts, criticizes, describes, discriminates, explains, justifies, interprets, relates, summarizes, supports

Table B.2   Major Categories in the Affective Domain of the Taxonomy of Educational Objectives

Descriptions of the Major Categories in the Affective Domain

1. **Receiving.** Receiving refers to the student's willingness to attend to particular phenomena or stimuli (classroom activities, textbook, music, etc.). From a teaching standpoint, it is concerned with getting, holding, and directing the student's attention. Learning outcomes in this area range from the simple awareness that a thing exists to selective attention on the part of the learner. Receiving represents the lowest level of learning outcomes in the affective domain.

2. **Responding.** Responding refers to active participation on the part of the student. At this level he or she not only attends to a particular phenomenon but also reacts to it in some way. Learning outcomes in this area may emphasize acquiescence in responding (reads assigned material), willingness to respond (voluntarily reads beyond assignment), or satisfaction in responding (reads for pleasure or enjoyment). The higher levels of this category include those instructional objectives that are commonly classified under "interest"; that is, those that stress the seeking out and enjoyment of particular activities.

3. **Valuing.** Valuing is concerned with the worth or value a student attaches to a particular object, phenomenon, or behavior. This ranges in degree from the more simple acceptance of a value (desires to improve group skills) to the more complex level of commitment (assumes responsibility for the effective functioning of the group). Valuing is based on the internalization of a set of specified values, but clues to these values are expressed in the student's overt behavior. Learning outcomes in this area are concerned with behavior that is consistent and stable enough to make the value clearly identifiable. Instructional objectives that are commonly classified under "attitudes" and "appreciation" would fall into this category.

4. **Organization.** Organization is concerned with bringing together different values, resolving conflicts between them, and beginning the building of an internally consistent value system. Thus the emphasis is on comparing, relating, and synthesizing values. Learning outcomes may be concerned with the conceptualization of a value (recognizes the responsibility of each individual for improving human relations) or with the organization of a value system (develops a vocational plan that satisfies his or her need for both economic security and social service). Instructional objectives relating to the development of a philosophy of life would fall into this category.

5. **Characterization by a Value or Value Complex.** At this level of the affective domain the individual has a value system that has controlled his or her behavior for a sufficiently long time for him or her to have developed a characteristic "lifestyle." Thus the behavior is pervasive, consistent, and predictable. Learning outcomes at this level cover a broad range of activities, but the major emphasis is on the fact that the behavior is typical or characteristic of the student. Instructional objectives that are concerned with the student's general patterns of adjustment (personal, social, emotional) would be appropriate here.

Illustrative General Instructional Objectives	Illustrative Verbs for Stating Specific Learning Outcomes
Listens attentively Shows awareness of the importance of learning Shows sensitivity to human needs and social problems Accepts differences of race and culture Attends closely to the classroom activities	Asks, chooses, describes, follows, gives, holds, identifies, locates, names, points to, replies, selects, sits erect, uses
Completes assigned homework Obeys school rules Participates in class discussion Completes laboratory work Volunteers for special tasks Shows interest in subject Enjoys helping others	Answers, assists, complies, conforms, discusses, greets, helps, labels, performs, practices, presents, reads, recites, reports, selects, tells, writes
Demonstrates belief in the democratic process Appreciates good literature (art or music) Appreciates the role of science (or other subjects) in everyday life Shows concern for the welfare of others Demonstrates problem-solving attitude Demonstrates commitment to social improvement	Completes, describes, differentiates, explains, follows, forms, initiates, invites, joins, justifies, proposes, reads, reports, selects, shares, studies, works
Recognizes the need for balance between freedom and responsibility in a democracy Recognizes the role of systematic planning in solving problems Accepts responsibility for his or her own behavior Understands and accepts his or her own strengths and limitations Formulates life plan in harmony with his or her abilities, interests, and beliefs	Adheres, alters, arranges, combines, compares, completes, defends, explains, generalizes, identifies, integrates, modifies, orders, organizes, prepares, relates, synthesizes
Displays safety consciousness Demonstrates self-reliance working independently Practices cooperation in group activities Uses objective approach in problem solving Demonstrates industry, punctuality, and self discipline Maintains good health habits	Acts, discriminates, displays, influences, listens, modifies, performs, practices, proposes, qualifies, questions, revises, serves, solves, uses, verifies

Table B.3   A Classification of Educational Objectives in the Psychomotor Domain

---

Descriptions of the Major Categories in the Psychomotor Domain

1. **Perception.** The first level is concerned with the use of the sense organs to obtain cues that guide motor activity. This category ranges from sensory stimulation (awareness of a stimulus), through cue selection (selecting task-relevant cues), to translation (relating cue perception to action in a performance).

2. **Set.** Set refers to readiness to take a particular type of action. This category includes mental set (mental readiness to act), physical set (physical readiness to act), and emotional set (willingness to act). Perception of cues serves as an important prerequisite for this level.

3. **Guided Response.** Guided response is concerned with the early stages in learning a complex skill. It includes imitation (repeating an act demonstrated by the instructor) and trial and error (using a multiple-response approach to identify an appropriate response). Adequacy of performance is judged by an instructor or by a suitable set of criteria.

4. **Mechanism.** Mechanism is concerned with performance acts where the learned responses have become habitual and the movements can be performed with some confidence and proficiency. Learning outcomes at this level are concerned with performance skills of various types, but the movement patterns are less complex than at the next higher level.

5. **Complex Overt Response.** Complex overt response is concerned with the skillful performance of motor acts that involve complex movement patterns. Proficiency is indicated by a quick, smooth, accurate performance, requiring a minimum of energy. This category includes resolution of uncertainty (performs without hesitation) and automatic performance (movements are made with ease and good muscle control). Learning outcomes at this level include highly coordinated motor activities.

6. **Adaptation.** Adaptation is concerned with skills that are so well developed that the individual can modify movement patterns to fit special requirements or to meet a problem situation.

7. **Origination.** Origination refers to the creating of new movement patterns to fit a particular situation or specific problem. Learning outcomes at this level emphasize creativity based upon highly developed skills.

Note: Material in first column from *The Classification of Educational Objectives in the Psychomotor Domain*, by E. J. Simpson, 1972, Washington, DC: Gryphon House, used by permission of the publisher. (Adapted by Simpson from David R. Krathwohl, Benjamin S. Bloom & Bertram B. Masia, *Taxonomy of Educational Objectives, Book 2: Affective Domain*. Published by Allyn and Bacon, Boston, MA. Copyright © 1964 by Pearson Education. Adapted with permission.)

Illustrative General Instructional Objectives	Illustrative Verbs for Stating Specific Learning Outcomes
Recognizes malfunction by sound of machine Relates taste of food to need for seasoning Relates music to a particular dance step	Chooses, describes, detects, differentiates, distinguishes, identifies, isolates, relates, selects, separates
Knows sequence of steps in varnishing wood Demonstrates proper bodily stance for batting a ball Shows desire to type efficiently	Begins, displays, explains, moves, proceeds, reacts, responds, shows, starts, volunteers
Performs a golf swing as demonstrated Applies first-aid bandage as demonstrated Determines best sequence for preparing a meal	Assembles, builds, calibrates, constructs, dismantles, displays, dissects, fastens, fixes, grinds, heats, manipulates, measures, mends, mixes, organizes, sketches, works
Writes smoothly and legibly Sets up laboratory equipment Operates a slide projector Demonstrates a simple dance step	(Same list as for Guided Response)
Operates a power saw skillfully Demonstrates correct form in swimming Demonstrates skill in driving an automobile Performs skillfully on the violin Repairs electronic equipment quickly and accurately	(Same list as for Guided Response)
Adjusts tennis play to counteract opponent's style Modifies swimming strokes to fit the roughness of the water	Adapts, alters, changes, rearranges, reorganizes, revises, varies
Creates a dance step Creates a musical composition Designs a new dress style	Arranges, combines, composes, constructs, designs, originates

Appendix C

Revised Taxonomy of Educational Objectives

Table C.1   The Major Types and Subtypes of the Knowledge Dimension

Major Types and Subtypes	Examples
A. Factual knowledge—The basic elements students must know to be acquainted with a discipline or solve problems in it	
Aa. Knowledge of terminology	Technical vocabulary, musical symbols
Ab. Knowledge of specific details and elements	Major natural resources, reliable sources of information
B. Conceptual knowledge—The interrelationships among the basic elements within a larger structure that enable them to function together	
Ba. Knowledge of classifications and categories	Periods of geological time, forms of business ownership
Bb. Knowledge of principles and generalizations	Pythagorean theorem, law of supply and demand
Bc. Knowledge of theories, models, and structures	Theory of evolution, structure of Congress
C. Procedural knowledge—How to do something, methods of inquiry, and criteria for using skills, algorithms, techniques, and methods	
Ca. Knowledge of subject-specific skills and algorithms	Skills used in painting with watercolors, whole-number division algorithm
Cb. Knowledge of subject-specific techniques and methods	Interviewing techniques, scientific method
Cc. Knowledge of criteria for determining when to use appropriate procedures	Criteria used to determine when to apply a procedure involving Newton's second law, criteria used to judge the feasibility of using a particular method to estimate business costs
D. Metacognitive knowledge—Knowledge of cognition in general as well as awareness and knowledge of one's own cognition	
Da. Strategic knowledge	Knowledge of outlining as a means of capturing the structure of a unit of subject matter in a textbook, knowledge of the use of heuristics
Db. Knowledge about cognitive tasks, including appropriate contextual and conditional knowledge	Knowledge of the types of tests particular teachers administer, knowledge of the cognitive demands of different tasks
Dc. Self-knowledge	Knowledge that critiquing essays is a personal strength, whereas writing essays is a personal weakness; awareness of one's own knowledge level

Table C.2   The Six Categories of the Cognitive Process Dimension and Related Cognitive Processes

Process Categories	Cognitive Processes and Examples
1. Remember—Retrieve relevant knowledge from long-term memory.	
1.1 **Recognizing**	(e.g., Recognize the dates of important events in U.S. history)
1.2 **Recalling**	(e.g., Recall the dates of important events in U.S. history)
2. Understand—Construct meaning from instructional messages, including oral, written, and graphic communication.	
2.1 **Interpreting**	(e.g., Paraphrase important speeches and documents)
2.2 **Exemplifying**	(e.g., Give examples of various artistic painting styles)
2.3 **Classifying**	(e.g., Classify observed or described cases of mental disorders)
2.4 **Summarizing**	(e.g., Write a short summary of the events portrayed on videotapes)
2.5 **Inferring**	(e.g., In learning a foreign language, infer grammatical principles from examples)
2.6 **Comparing**	(e.g., Compare historical events to contemporary situations)
2.7 **Explaining**	(e.g., Explain the causes of important eighteenth-century events in France)
3. Apply—Carry out or use a procedure in a given situation.	
3.1 **Executing**	(e.g., Divide one whole number by another whole number, both with multiple digits)
3.2 **Implementing**	(e.g., Determine in which situations Newton's second law is appropriate)
4. Analyze—Break material into constituent parts and determine how parts relate to one another and to an overall structure or purpose.	
4.1 **Differentiating**	(e.g., Distinguish between relevant and irrelevant numbers in a mathematical word problem)
4.2 **Organizing**	(e.g., Structure evidence in a historical description into evidence for and against a particular historical explanation)
4.3 **Attributing**	(e.g., Determine the point of view of the author of an essay in terms of his or her political perspective)
5. Evaluate—Make judgments based on criteria and standards.	
5.1 **Checking**	(e.g., Determine whether a scientist's conclusions follow from observed data)
5.2 **Critiquing**	(e.g., Judge which of two methods is the best way to solve a given problem)
6. Create—Put elements together to form a coherent or functional whole; reorganize elements into a new pattern or structure.	
6.1 **Generating**	(e.g., Generate hypotheses to account for an observed phenomenon)
6.2 **Planning**	(e.g., Plan a research paper on a given historical topic)
6.3 **Producing**	(e.g., Build habitats for certain species for certain purposes)

Table C.3   How an Objective (The Student Will Learn to Apply the Reduce-Reuse-Recycle Approach to Conservation) Is Classified in the Taxonomy Table

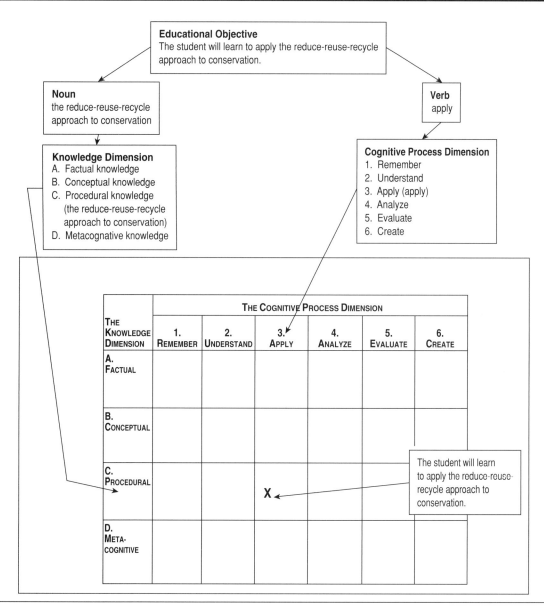

Appendix D

Depth-of-Knowledge by Subject Descriptors

Depth of Knowledge

Subject	Level 1	Level 2	Level 3	Level 4
English Language Arts	Requires students to recall, observe, question, or represent facts or simple skills or abilities. Requires only surface understanding of text, often verbatim recall. Examples: • Support ideas by reference to details in text • Use dictionary to find meaning • Identify figurative language in passage • Identify correct spelling or meaning of words	Requires processing beyond recall and observation. Requires both comprehension and subsequent processing of text. Involves ordering, classifying text as well as identifying patterns, relationships, and main points. Examples: • Use context to identify unfamiliar words • Predict logical outcome • Identify and summarize main points • Apply knowledge of conventions of standard American English • Compose accurate summaries	Requires students to go beyond text. Requires students to explain, generalize, and connect ideas. Involves inferencing, prediction, elaboration, and summary. Requires students to support positions using prior knowledge and to manipulate themes across passages. Examples: • Determine effect of author's purpose on text elements • Summarize information from multiple sources • Critically analyze literature • Compose focused, organized, coherent, purposeful prose	Requires extended higher order processing. Typically requires extended time to complete task, but time spent not on repetitive tasks. Involves taking information from one text/passage and applying this information to a new task. May require generating hypotheses and performing complex analyses and connections among texts. Examples: • Analyze and synthesize information from multiple sources • Examine and explain alternative perspectives across sources • Describe and illustrate common themes across a variety of texts • Create compositions that synthesize, analyze, and evaluate

Depth of Knowledge

Subject	Level 1	Level 2	Level 3	Level 4
Mathematics	Requires students to recall or observe facts, definitions, terms. Involves simple one-step procedures. Involves computing simple algorithms (e.g., sum, quotient) Examples: • Recall or recognize a fact, term, or property • Represent in words, pictures, or symbols a math object or relationship • Perform routine procedure, such as measuring	Requires students to make decisions on how to approach a problem. Requires students to compare, classify, organize, estimate, or order data. Typically involves two-step procedures. Examples: • Specify and explain relationships between facts, terms, properties, or operations • Select procedure according to criteria and perform it • Solve routine multiple-step problems	Requires reasoning, planning, or use of evidence to solve problem or algorithm. May involve activity with more than one possible answer. Requires conjecture or restructuring of problems. Involves drawing conclusions from observations, citing evidence and developing logical arguments for concepts. Uses concepts to solve non-routine problems. Examples: • Analyze similarities and differences • Formulate original problem given situation • Formulate mathematical model for complex situation	Requires complex reasoning, planning, developing, and thinking. Typically requires extended time to complete problem, but time spent not on repetitive tasks. Requires students to make several connections and apply one approach among many to solve the problem. Involves complex restructuring of data, establishing and evaluating criteria to solve problems. Examples: • Apply mathematical model to illuminate a problem, situation • Conduct a project that specifies a problem, identifies solution paths, solves the problem, and reports results • Design a mathematical model to inform and solve a practical or abstract situation

Depth of Knowledge

Subject	Level 1	Level 2	Level 3	Level 4
Science	Requires students to recall facts, definitions, or simple procedures or processes. Involves rote responses, use of well-known formulae, or following a set of clearly defined one-step procedures. Examples: • Recall or recognize a fact, term, or property • Represent in words or diagrams a scientific concept or relationship • Provide or recognize a standard scientific representation or simple phenomenon	Requires students to make some decisions as to how to approach the question or problem. Involves comparing, classifying, organizing, estimating, ordering, or displaying data (e.g., tables, graphs, charts). Typically involves multiple-step procedures. Examples: • Specify and explain the relationship between facts, terms, properties, or variables • Describe and explain examples and non-examples of science concepts • Select a procedure according to specified criteria and perform it	Requires students to solve problems with more than one possible answer and justify responses. Experimental design involves more than one dependent variable. Requires drawing conclusions from observations, citing evidence, and developing logical argument for concepts; explaining phenomena in terms of concepts, and using concepts to solve non-routine problems. Examples: • Identify research questions and design investigations for a scientific problem • Develop a scientific model for a complex situation • Form conclusions from experimental data	Requires students to make several connections and apply one approach among many to solve problems. Involves developing generalizations from obtained results and formulating strategies to solve new problems in a variety of situations. Requires extended time to complete problem, but time spent not on repetitive tasks. Examples: • Based on provided data from a complex experiment that is novel to the student, deduce the fundamental relationship between several controlled variables • Conduct an investigation, from specifying a problem to designing and carrying out an experiment, to analyzing its data and formulating conclusions

Depth of Knowledge

Subject	Level 1	Level 2	Level 3	Level 4
Social Studies	Requires students to recall facts (who, what, when, and where), terms, concepts, trends, generalizations, and theories or to recognize or identify specific information contained in maps, charts, tables, graphs, or drawings. Examples: • Recall or recognize an event, map, or document • Describe the features of a place or people • Identify key figures in a particular context	Requires students to compare or contrast people, places, events, and concepts; give examples, classify or sort items into meaningful categories; describe, interpret or explain issues and problems, patterns, reasons, causes, effects, significance or impact, relationships, and points of view or processes. Examples: • Describe the causes/ effects of particular events • Identify patterns in events or behavior • Categorize events or figures into meaningful groupings	Requires students to draw conclusions, cite evidence, apply concepts to new situations; use concepts to solve problems, analyze similarities and differences in issues and problems; propose and evaluate solutions; recognize and explain misconceptions; make connections and explain main concepts. Examples: • Analyze how changes have affected people or places • Apply concepts in other contexts • Form alternate conclusions	Requires students to connect and relate ideas and concepts within and among content areas. Involves analyzing and synthesizing information from multiple sources; examining and explaining alternative perspectives across a variety of sources; making predictions with evidence as support; planning and developing solutions to problems. Examples: • Given a situation/problem research, define and describe the situation/ problem and provide alternative solutions • Describe, define and illustrate common social, historical, or geographical themes and how they interrelate

Source: Webb, N. L. (2002). *Alignment study in language arts, mathematics, science and social studies of state standards and assessments for four states.* Washington, DC: Council of Chief State School Officers. Adapted with permission from Figure 1, pp. 9–12.

Appendix E

Illustrative Verbs

Illustrative Verbs for Stating General Instructional Objectives

Analyze	Compute	Interpret	Perform	Translate
Apply	Create	Know	Recognize	Understand
Appreciate	Demonstrate	Listen	Speak	Use
Comprehend	Evaluate	Locate	Think	Write

Illustrative Verbs for Stating Specific Learning Outcomes[1]

"Creative" Behaviors

Alter	Paraphrase	Reconstruct	Rephrase	Rewrite
Ask	Predict	Regroup	Restate	Simplify
Change	Question	Rename	Restructure	Synthesize
Design	Rearrange	Reorder	Retell	Systematize
Generalize	Recombine	Reorganize	Revise	Vary
Modify				

Complex, Logical, Judgmental Behaviors

Analyze	Conclude	Deduce	Formulate	Plan
Appraise	Contrast	Defend	Generate	Structure
Combine	Criticize	Evaluate	Induce	Substitute
Compare	Decide	Explain	Infer	

---

[1] This list was developed by Calvin K. Claus, Psychology Department, National College of Education, Evanston, IL. Printed by permission from a paper presented at the annual meeting of the National Council on Measurement in Education (Chicago: February, 1968). It provides a useful collection of verbs for the beginner.

General Discriminative Behaviors

Choose	Detect	Identify	Match	Place
Collect	Differentiate	Indicate	Omit	Point
Define	Discriminate	Isolate	Order	Select
Describe	Distinguish	List	Pick	Separate

Social Behaviors

Accept	Communicate	Discuss	Invite	Praise
Agree	Compliment	Excuse	Join	React
Aid	Contribute	Forgive	Laugh	Smile
Allow	Cooperate	Greet	Meet	Talk
Answer	Dance	Help	Participate	Thank
Argue	Disagree	Interact	Permit	Volunteer

Language Behaviors

Abbreviate	Edit	Punctuate	Speak	Tell
Accent	Hyphenate	Read	Spell	Translate
Alphabetize	Indent	Recite	State	Verbalize
Articulate	Outline	Say	Summarize	Whisper
Call	Print	Sign	Syllabify	Write
Capitalize	Pronounce			

"Study" Behaviors

Arrange	Compile	Itemize	Mark	Record
Categorize	Copy	Label	Name	Reproduce
Chart	Diagram	Locate	Note	Search
Circle	Find	Look	Organize	Sort
Cite	Follow	Map	Quote	Underline

Music Behaviors

Blow	Compose	Hum	Pluck	Strum
Bow	Finger	Mute	Practice	Tap
Clap	Harmonize	Play	Sing	Whistle

Physical Behaviors

Arch	Catch	Float	Hit	Knock
Bat	Chase	Grab	Hop	Lift
Bend	Climb	Grasp	Jump	March

Carry	Face	Grip	Kick	Pitch
Pull	Skate	Somersault	Stretch	Throw
Push	Ski	Stand	Swim	Toss
Run	Skip	Step	Swing	Walk

Arts Behaviors

Assemble	Dot	Illustrate	Press	Stamp
Blend	Draw	Melt	Roll	Stick
Brush	Drill	Mix	Rub	Stir
Build	Fold	Mold	Sand	Trace
Carve	Form	Nail	Saw	Trim
Color	Frame	Paint	Sculpt	Varnish
Construct	Hammer	Paste	Shake	Wipe
Cut	Handle	Pat	Sketch	Wrap
Dab	Heat	Pour	Smooth	

Drama Behaviors

Act	Display	Express	Pass	Show
Clasp	Emit	Leave	Perform	Sit
Cross	Enter	Move	Proceed	Start
Direct	Exit	Pantomime	Respond	Turn

Mathematical Behaviors

Add	Derive	Group	Number	Square
Bisect	Divide	Integrate	Plot	Subtract
Calculate	Estimate	Interpolate	Prove	Tabulate
Check	Extract	Measure	Reduce	Tally
Compute	Extrapolate	Multiply	Solve	Verify
Count	Graph			

Laboratory Science Behaviors

Apply	Demonstrate	Keep	Prepare	Specify
Calibrate	Dissect	Lengthen	Remove	Straighten
Conduct	Feed	Limit	Replace	Time
Connect	Grow	Manipulate	Report	Transfer
Convert	Increase	Operate	Reset	Weigh
Decrease	Insert	Plant	Set	

General Appearance, Health, and Safety Behaviors

Button	Dress	Fasten	Taste	Unzip
Clean	Drink	Fill	Tie	Wait
Clear	Eat	Go	Unbutton	Wash
Close	Eliminate	Lace	Uncover	Wear
Comb	Empty	Stop	Untie	Zip
Cover				

Miscellaneous

Aim	Erase	Lead	Relate	Stake
Attempt	Expand	Lend	Repeat	Start
Attend	Extend	Let	Return	Stock
Begin	Feel	Light	Ride	Store
Bring	Finish	Make	Rip	Strike
Buy	Fit	Mend	Save	Suggest
Come	Fix	Miss	Scratch	Supply
Complete	Flip	Offer	Send	Support
Consider	Get	Open	Serve	Switch
Correct	Give	Pack	Sew	Take
Crease	Grind	Pay	Share	Tear
Crush	Guide	Peel	Sharpen	Touch
Designate	Hand	Pin	Shoot	Try
Determine	Hang	Position	Shorten	Twist
Develop	Hold	Present	Shovel	Type
Discover	Hook	Produce	Shut	Use
Distribute	Hunt	Propose	Signify	Vote
Do	Include	Provide	Slide	Watch
Drop	Inform	Put	Slip	Weave
End	Lay	Raise	Spread	Work

Appendix F

Answers to Exercises

Chapter 1

1. Specifying intended learning *outcomes* means stating what the student should understand or be able to do as a result of instruction. This helps you plan the procedures you will use in instruction because it keeps you (and the student) focused on the target they are trying to hit. Often, many different instructional procedures could be used to help students reach intended learning outcomes—and sometimes, different instruction works better for different students. The point is what they can do when they have learned.

2. Stating the general instructional objective first and then clarifying it further by listing the specific types of performance that characterize that objective makes clear that the general instructional objective (e.g., comprehension) is the goal of instruction. This will help you focus your teaching on understanding and not atomistic performance of a list of "to-dos." The specific learning outcomes just describe a sample of the types of performance that represent achievement of the general instructional objective. For many general instructional objectives, a different sample of specific types of performance could serve equally well. The specific outcomes are necessary so that you and the student recognize what you will take as evidence of achievement of the general objective. They also help clarify the meaning of the general objective.

Chapter 2

1. General instructional objectives

    a. "Applies rounding rules" is better because a general instructional objective should specify an intended learning *outcome*. "Applying" is an outcome, and "learns" is a process.

    b. "Comprehends the plot of a novel" is better for the same reason. "Comprehends" is an outcome, and "reads" is a process.

2. Specific learning outcomes

    a. "Predicts the outcome of an experiment" is better. "Predicts" is an observable outcome, and "Does an experiment" is a process.

b. "Applies a principle to solve problems" is better in most cases (there could be exceptions for certain classes or individual students). In this example, both choices are observable outcomes, but the first is a rote performance, and the second is a higher-level performance.

Chapter 3

1. Use instructional objectives

   a. To plan for instruction by selecting teaching methods and materials congruent with the general instructional objective, including *but not limited to* the kinds of activities in the specific learning outcomes.

   b. To plan for formative assessment by building ongoing checks on student progress congruent with the general instructional objective, including *but not limited to* the kinds of activities in the specific learning outcomes.

   c. To plan for summative assessment by creating or selecting assessments based on the specific learning outcomes.

   d. To share with students, either directly or through assignments and instructional activities that clearly embody the instructional objectives. This helps students see where they are supposed to be going and regulate their own learning.

2. Answers will vary. Most students will produce an instructional planning chart similar to Table 3.1 or 3.2. Evaluate the chart by this checklist:

   _____ Do assignments match the instructional objective?

   _____ Do instructional activities match the instructional objective?

   _____ Do assessment activities match the instructional objective?

   _____ Are the assignments and instructional activities sufficient to produce the intended learning outcomes for most students?

Chapter 4

1. Answers will vary. Evaluate answers with this rubric.

   _____ Does the answer report on 2 states besides those in the chapter?

   2 = completely and clearly, 1 = partially, 0 = no

   _____ Does the discussion reasonably compare and contrast the 2 new states' examples with the chapter examples and conclusions that there is great variability in the specificity and organization of state standards?

   4 = completely and clearly, 2 = partially, 0 = no

2. Answers will vary. Evaluate the examples with Checklist items 6 to 18 (for General Instructional Objectives and Specific Learning Outcomes) in Appendix A.

Chapter 5

1. Ms. Jones should point out that a frame of reference or taxonomy of learning outcomes can (a) help you identify learning outcomes, (b) help you articulate them in

writing, (c) help you organize objectives into appropriate lists, and (d) help you consider the whole range of learning outcomes (so you don't miss something).

2. Answers will vary. Evaluate the examples with Checklist items 6 to 18 (for General Instructional Objectives and Specific Learning Outcomes) in Appendix A. Apply conventions of standard written English (e.g. Spelling, punctuation, usage) appropriate for grade level and purpose Apply conventions of standard written English (e.g. Spelling, punctuation, usage) appropriate for grade level and purpose Apply conventions of standard written English (e.g. Spelling, punctuation, usage) appropriate for grade level and purpose

Chapter 6

1. Answers will vary. Evaluate answers with this rubric.

_____ Do the general instructional objectives for the three levels either come from Figure 6.1, or are they a reasonable adaptation that preserves the appropriate cognitive level?

3 = all 3, 2 = 2 of 3, 1 = 1 of 3, 0 = no

_____ Do the specific learning outcomes exemplify the characteristics in Checklist items 13 to 18 (for Specific Learning Outcomes) in Appendix A?

6 = completely, 3 = partially, 0 = no

_____ Are the specific learning outcomes at the appropriate level for lower primary students?

2 = completely, 1 = partially, 0 = no

2. Answers will vary. Evaluate answers with this rubric.

_____ Do the general instructional objectives for the three levels either come from Figure 6.1, or are they a reasonable adaptation that preserves the appropriate cognitive level?

3 = all 3, 2 = 2 of 3, 1 = 1 of 3, 0 = no

_____ Do the specific learning outcomes exemplify the characteristics in Checklist items 13 to 18 (for Specific Learning Outcomes) in Appendix A?

6 = completely, 3 = partially, 0 = no

_____ Are the specific learning outcomes at the appropriate level for upper secondary students?

2 = completely, 1 = partially, 0 = no

Chapter 7

1. Answers will vary. Good generic general instructional objectives will (a) be similar to the models on page 72 and (b) make appropriate use of suggested specific skills from Figures 7.1 and 7.2.

2. Answers will vary. Good answers will adapt the generic instructional objectives from Exercise 1 appropriately for the grade level and subject matter specified.

Chapter 8

1. Good answers will note at least two reasons affective objectives are hard to write: (a) we often use affective terms and concepts loosely, so the they are vague and hard to classify; and (b) evidence of students' internal dispositions and feelings is indirect (e.g., by inference or by self-report).

2. [No evaluation here—the point is to brainstorm as many specific affective outcomes about reading dispositions as possible, whether good or bad.]

3. Sorting the specific affective outcomes:

   a. Poor-quality outcomes will be statements that (a) require high levels of inference and/or (b) are subject to "teacher-pleasing" or socially acceptable responses. For example, "appears interested in the story" requires a high level of observer inference—it would be hard to agree on what that looks like. Or for example, if a student's reading teacher asks her if she likes to read, of course she is likely to say yes. This kind of specific outcome should be identified and set aside.

   b. Evaluate each of the two instructional objectives for "Shows interest in reading" with this checklist:

   _____ Do the specific outcomes match the instructional objective?

   _____ Is it clear how the specific outcomes could be assessed?

   _____ Are the specific outcomes appropriate to a lower primary reading class or an upper secondary English class (respectively)?

Chapter 9

Evaluate each of the three instructional objectives (for a procedure, a product, and both, respectively) with this checklist:

_____ Do the general objectives focus on an important procedure, a product, or both, respectively?

_____ Does the list of specific performance outcomes include the important aspects of the skill or product?

_____ Is the list of specific performance outcomes sufficient to describe successful performance?

_____ Are the specific performance outcomes stated as criteria for judging the performance?

_____ Are the specific performance outcomes stated in terms students can understand?

Chapter 10

1. Answers will vary. Good answers will follow the model specified and describe a restricted problem-solving project appropriate to the instructional area of interest.

2. Answers will vary. Good answers will follow the model specified and describe an extended problem-solving project appropriate to the instructional area of interest.

3. A good critique will address each of the questions completely and clearly. If the answer to any of the questions is "no" or "not very well," a good critique will make suggestions for improvement.

   a. Is the objective written in such a way that students would understand it?

   b. Does the objective reflect a common and worthwhile problem in the instructional area?

   c. Does the objective provide clear criteria for judging the performance?

Chapter 11

1. A good answer will make the following points in the context of the content area and grade level of interest. (a) General instructional objectives identify the achievement to be tested. (b) Specific learning outcomes define that achievement in observable, measurable terms. (c) The general instructional objectives provide the column headings for an achievement test's table of specifications. (d) The specific learning outcomes may help with the writing of the test items by suggesting specifics for the questions.

2. A test's table of specifications is a matrix that crosses the general instructional objectives (usually the columns) with a content outline (usually the rows). The matrix allows for planning the number of questions for each cell. The result should be a plan that leads directly to the construction of a test which reflects learning outcomes across the intended range of content and thinking skills for the unit of instruction.

Chapter 12

1. Answers will vary. Good answers will have selected one of the specified instructional objectives from the text.

   a. Good checklists use the list of specific learning outcomes and supply a line for writing yes/no or a box for making a check.

   b. Good rating scales or rubrics use the list of specific learning outcomes and supply a scale that allows indications of the quality of performance. The scale's points will be labeled with text appropriate to the performance being evaluated.

   c. The scales in (a) and (b) are analytic because a judgment was provided for each criterion (as opposed to one overall judgment).

2. Answers will vary. Good answers will have selected one of the specified affective objectives from the text.

   a. Good checklists use the list of specific affective outcomes and supply a line for writing yes/no or a box for making a check.

   b. Good rating scales use the list of specific learning outcomes and supply a scale that allows indications of quality or intensity. The scale's points will be labeled with text appropriate to the affective characteristic being evaluated.

   c. For most affective objectives, the rating scale will be more appropriate because affective outcomes most often are a matter of degree rather than all-or-nothing. However, for some objectives (e.g., a list of safety procedures), a checklist may be more appropriate.

References

Anderson, L. W., & Bourke, S. F. (2000). *Assessing affective characteristics in the schools* (2nd ed.). Mahwah, NJ: Lawrence Erlbaum Associates.

Describes and illustrates how to construct measures of affective characteristics.

Anderson, L. W., & Krathwohl, D. R. (Eds.). (2001). *A taxonomy for teaching, learning, and assessing.* New York: Longman.

Presents a revision of Bloom's Taxonomy of Educational Objectives.

Arter, J. A., & McTighe, J. (2001). *Scoring rubrics in the classroom: Using performance criteria for assessing and improving student performance.* Thousand Oaks, CA: Corwin Press.

Describes how to use performance criteria for clarifying the goals of instruction and improving the assessment of student learning.

Bloom, B. S. (Ed.), Englehart, M. D., Furst, E. J., Hill, W. H., & Krathwohl, D. R. (1956). *Taxonomy of educational objectives: Handbook I: Cognitive domain.* New York: David McKay.

Describes the cognitive categories in detail and presents illustrative objectives and test items for each.

Brookhart, S. M., & Nitko, A. J. (2008). *Assessment and grading in classrooms.* Upper Saddle River, NJ: Pearson Prentice Hall.

Presents a basic introduction to educational assessment with a focus on the classroom.

Gronlund, N. E. (2006). *Assessment of student achievement* (8th ed.). Boston: Allyn and Bacon.

Describes and illustrates how to construct test items and various procedures used in assessing student learning.

Harrow, A. J. (1972). *A taxonomy of the psychomotor domain.* New York: David McKay.

Provides a model for classifying learning outcomes in the psychomotor domain and presents illustrative objectives.

Kendall, J. S., & Marzano, R. J. (2004). *Content knowledge: A compendium of standards and benchmarks for K–12 education.* Aurora, CO: Mid-continent Research for Education and Learning. Online database: http://www.mcrel.org/standards-benchmarks/

Comprehensive lists of standards and benchmarks in all major subjects.

Krathwohl, D. R., Bloom, B. S., & Masia, B. B. (1964). *Taxonomy of educational objectives: Handbook II: Affective domain.* New York: David McKay.

Describes the affective categories in detail and presents illustrative objectives and test items for each.

Marzano, R. J., & Kendall, J. S. (2007). *The new taxonomy of educational objectives* (2nd ed.). Thousand Oaks, CA: Corwin Press.

>   Describes a taxonomy that incorporates how the mind works, the nature of knowledge, and an interaction of the two: an alternative to the Anderson and Krathwohl revision of Bloom's Taxonomy.

Nitko, A. J., & Brookhart, S. M. (2007). *Educational assessment of students* (5th ed.). Upper Saddle River, NJ: Pearson Prentice Hall.

>   Presents a comprehensive introduction to educational assessment.

Simpson, E. J. (1972). The classification of educational objectives in the psychomotor domain. *The psychomotor domain* (Vol. 3). Washington, DC: Gryphon House.

>   Describes the psychomotor domain in detail and presents illustrative objectives.

Smith, J. K., Smith, L. F., and DeLisa, R. (2001). *Natural classroom assessment.* Thousand Oaks, CA: Corwin Press.

>   A practical approach to preparing and using assessments that facilitate the teaching–learning process.

Webb, N. L. (2002). *Alignment study in language arts, mathematics, science, and social studies of state standards and assessments for four states.* Washington, DC: Council of Chief State School Officers.

>   Describes the method and results for several studies of the alignment between state standards and assessments. Includes a description of a framework for classifying the Depth of Knowledge of standards and assessments. Also see:

Webb, N. L. (2007). Issues related to judging the alignment of curriculum standards and assessments. *Applied Measurement in Education, 20,* 7–25.

Index